THE
BROTHER/SISTER
PLAYS

THE
BROTHER/SISTER
PLAYS

Tarell Alvin McCraney

THEATRE COMMUNICATIONS GROUP
NEW YORK
2010

The Brother/Sister Plays is published by Theatre Communications Group, Inc., 520 Eighth Avenue, 24th Floor, New York, NY 10018–4156

This publication is made possible in part with public funds from the New York State Council on the Arts, a State Agency.

TCG books are exclusively distributed to the book trade by Consortium Book Sales and Distribution.

McCraney, Tarell Alvin.
The brother/sister plays / Tarell Alvin McCraney.
p. cm.
ISBN 978-1-55936-349-5
1. Brothers—Louisiana—Drama. 2. Female impersonators—Drama.
3. African American gay men—Drama. 4. Female impersonators—Drama.
5. Drag balls—Drama. 6. Nigerians—Louisiana—Drama.
7. Louisiana—Drama. I. Title.
PS3613.C38625B79   2010
812'.6—dc22   2010008792

Cover image by Loni Johnson
Text design and composition by Lisa Govan

First Edition, July 2010

Contents

The Brother/Sister Plays draws on elements, icons and stories from the Yoruba cosmology.

If there is no dialogue following a character's name, it means there is a silent action or pause being played at that moment.

The stage directions in a character's speech are meant to be said as well as played.

IN THE RED
AND BROWN WATER

A Fast and Loose Play on Spanish *Yerma*
and African Oya/Oba

To my sisters

The Brother/Sister Plays (*In the Red and Brown Water, The Brothers Size* and *Marcus; Or the Secret of Sweet*) were workshopped at the Yale School of Drama, the first and last plays of the trilogy premiering in Yale's first Carlotta Festival of New Plays in 2006. The trilogy then premiered in April 2009 at the McCarter Theatre Center (Emily Mann, Artistic Director/Resident Playwright; Timothy J. Shields, Managing Director) in Princeton, in association with The Public Theater (Oskar Eustis, Artistic Director; Andrew D. Hamingson, Managing Director) in New York City, where it was later produced in October 2009.

At the McCarter: *In the Red and Brown Water* was directed by Tina Landau; *The Brothers Size* and *Marcus; Or the Secret of Sweet* were directed by Robert O'Hara; the set design was by James Schuette, the costume design was by Karen Perry, the lighting design was by Jane Cox, the sound design was by Lindsay Jones; the producing director was Mara Isaacs, the production stage manager was Cheryl Mintz. The cast was as follows:

PART 1: *In the Red and Brown Water*

OYA	Kianné Muschett
ELEGBA	Alano Miller

OGUN SIZE	Marc Damon Johnson
MAMA MOJA, THE WOMAN WHO REMINDS YOU, NIA	Heather Alicia Simms
AUNT ELEGUA	Kimberly Hébert Gregory
SHUN	Nikiya Mathis
SHANGO	Samuel Ray Gates
THE MAN FROM STATE, O LI ROON	Barnaby Carpenter
EGUNGUN	Brian Tyree Henry

PART 2: *The Brothers Size*

OGUN SIZE	Marc Damon Johnson
OSHOOSI SIZE	Brian Tyree Henry
ELEGBA	Alano Miller

PART 3: *Marcus; Or the Secret of Sweet*

MARCUS	Alano Miller
OSHOOSI SIZE, TERRELL	Brian Tyree Henry
OBA	Heather Alicia Simms
OGUN SIZE	Marc Damon Johnson
OSHA	Kianné Muschett
SHAUNTA IYUN	Nikiya Mathis
SHUN, AUNT ELEGUA	Kimberly Hébert Gregory
SHUA	Samuel Ray Gates
O LI ROON	Barnaby Carpenter

In The Public Theater's production (October 2009), the trilogy was presented with the following changes: the lighting design was by Peter Kaczorowski, the music supervision and additional vocal arrangements were by Zane Mark; the production stage manager was Barbara Reo. The cast changes were as follows:

PART 1: *In the Red and Brown Water*

ELEGBA	André Holland
SHANGO	Sterling K. Brown
THE MAN FROM STATE, O LI ROON	Sean Allan Krill

PART 2: *The Brothers Size*

ELEGBA	André Holland

PART 3: *Marcus; Or the Secret of Sweet*

MARCUS	André Holland
SHUA	Sterling K. Brown
O LI ROON	Sean Allan Krill

The Brother/Sister Plays (*In the Red and Brown Water, The Brothers Size* and *Marcus; Or the Secret of Sweet*) was produced in January 2010 at Steppenwolf Theatre Company (Martha Lavey, Artistic Director; David Hawkanson, Executive Director) in Chicago. The director was Tina Landau; the set and costume design were by James Schuette, the lighting design was by Scott Zielinski, the sound design was by Rob Milburn and Michael Bodeen; the musical supervisor was Zane Mark, the fight choreographer was David Blixt, the stage manager was Deb Styer. The cast was as follows:

PART 1: *In the Red and Brown Water*

OYA	Alan Arenas
ELEGBA	Glenn Davis
OGUN SIZE	K. Todd Freeman
MAMA MOJA, THE WOMAN WHO REMINDS YOU, NIA	Ora Jones
AUNT ELEGUA	Jacqueline Williams

SHUN	Tamberla Perry
SHANGO	Rodrick Covington
THE MAN FROM STATE, O LI ROON	Jeff Parker
EGUNGUN	Phillip James Brannon

PART 2: *The Brothers Size*

OGUN SIZE	K. Todd Freeman
OSHOOSI SIZE	Phillip James Brannon
ELEGBA	Glenn Davis

PART 3: *Marcus; Or the Secret of Sweet*

MARCUS	Glenn Davis
OSHOOSI SIZE, TERRELL	Phillip James Brannon
OBA	Ora Jones
OGUN SIZE	K. Todd Freeman
OSHA	Tamberla Perry
SHAUNTA IYUN	Alan Arenas
SHUN, AUNT ELEGUA	Jacqueline Williams
SHUA	Rodrick Covington
O LI ROON	Jeff Parker

In the Red and Brown Water was produced in February 2008 at the Alliance Theatre (Susan V. Booth, Artistic Director; Thomas Pechar, Managing Director) in Atlanta. It was directed by Tina Landau; the set design was by Mimi Lien, the costume design was by Jessica Jahn, the lighting design was by Scott Zielinski, the sound design was by Mimi Epstein; the production stage manager was Pat A. Flora, the dramaturg was Celise Kalke. The cast was as follows:

OYA	Kianné Muschett
ELEGBA	Jon Michael Hill
OGUN SIZE	André Holland
MAMA MOJA, THE WOMAN WHO	
REMINDS YOU	Chinái J. Hardy
NIA	Sharisa Whatley
AUNT ELEGUA	Heather Alicia Simms
SHUN	Carra Patterson
SHANGO	Rodrick Covington
THE MAN FROM STATE, O LI ROON	Daniel Thomas May
EGUNGUN	Will Cobbs

In the Red and Brown Water was produced in October 2008 at the Young Vic in London. It was directed by Walter Meierjohann; the set design was by Miriam Buether, the costume supervision was by Iona Kenrick, the lighting design was by Jean Kalman, the sound design was by Fergus O'Hare, the music was by Abram Wilson; the stage manager was Susie Bourke. The cast was as follows:

OYA	Ony Uhiara
ELEGBA	John MacMillan
OGUN SIZE	Javone Prince
MAMA MOJA, THE WOMAN WHO	
REMINDS YOU	Adjoa Andoh
NIA	Sheri-An Davis
AUNT ELEGUA	Cecilia Noble
SHUN	Camilla Beeput
SHANGO	Ashley Walters
THE MAN FROM STATE, O LI ROON	Paul Thornley
EGUNGUN	Abram Wilson

In the Red and Brown Water was produced in January 2010 by The Studio Theatre (Joy Zinoman, Founding Artistic Director; Keith Alan Baker, Managing Director/Artistic Director, 2nd Stage) in Washington, D.C. It was directed by Serge Seiden; the set design was by Luciana Stecconi, the costume design was by Reggie Ray, the lighting design was by Michael Giannitti, the sound design was by Eric Shimelonis; the dramaturg was Sarah Wallace, the production stage manager was John Keith Hall. The cast was as follows:

OYA	Raushanah Simmons
ELEGBA	Mark Hairston
OGUN SIZE	Jahi A. Kearse
MAMA MOJA, THE WOMAN WHO REMINDS YOU	Denise Diggs
NIA	Shaunté Corrina Tabb
AUNT ELEGUA	Deidra LaWan Starnes
SHUN	Shannon Alexandria Lillie Dorsey
SHANGO	Yaegel T. Welch
THE MAN FROM STATE, O LI ROON	Michael Harris
EGUNGUN	Ricardo Frederick Evans

CHARACTERS

OYA	begins the play a girl and ends it a woman; a woman of color
ELEGBA	begins the play a boy and ends it a man, godbrother to Oya; of Creole heritage
OGUN SIZE	with Oya for a time, nephew of Aunt Elegua; a man of color
MAMA MOJA, THE WOMAN WHO REMINDS YOU	mother of Oya, godmother to Elegba; a mother of color
AUNT ELEGUA	aunt to Ogun, godmother to Oya; a woman of color
NIA	girl from around the way
SHUN	girl from around the way, friend to Nia; a fair woman of color
SHANGO	with Oya for a time; a dark man of color
THE MAN FROM STATE, O LI ROON	a white man
EGUNGUN	a DJ, a boy from around the way

TIME

Distant present

PLACE

San Pere, Louisiana

PROLOGUE

The lights come up.
The cast is standing in a line downstage.
The men all begin to hum, a sad sweet hum,
Thick like the early morning mist.
They move upstage.
Halfway through the journey
Oya is left center stage, alone.
She lies down on the ground, holds her head
And stares up to the sky. Her lines are said from this position
    like a chant or moan.
The others continue upstage, speaking their lines, the men
    still humming.
Until finally they stand still.
The cast glows like a pantheon of deities, ending the
    Prologue.

OYA

(Sharp breath out)
Ah!

AUNT ELEGUA

I don't know all . . .

MAMA MOJA

Nobody does.

AUNT ELEGUA

But say she ain't even scream.

OYA

Oya in the air Oya . . .

SHUN

Say it sound like the wind . . .

MAMA MOJA

Like a breeze . . .

OYA

A breeze over Oya.

SHUN

That's what they say?

MAMA MOJA, AUNT ELEGUA AND SHUN

Huh.

OYA

Oya . . . Oya . . .

AUNT ELEGUA

She enters.

OYA

Oya.

MAMA MOJA

Holding her head.

OYA

Oya gal . . .

SHUN

Laying up somewhere.

MAMA MOJA

Staring out somewhere.

MAMA MOJA, AUNT ELEGUA AND SHUN

Somewhere . . .

ALL

Huh.

MAMA MOJA

Lord God . . .

OYA

Oya . . .

SHUN

That girl

OYA

Oya.

AUNT ELEGUA

Sweet smiling

OYA

Oya in the air . . .

MAMA MOJA

Sad in the eyes

OYA

In the air . . . Oya

AUNT ELEGUA

That's what they say.

SHUN

That's what I know . . .

OYA

Oya.

AUNT ELEGUA

Beautiful girl.

ACT 1

SCENE 1

                              MAMA MOJA
Mama Moja enters the space . . .
Where you going Oya?

                                 OYA
Gotta go. Track meet.

                              MAMA MOJA
No.

                                 OYA
No?

                              MAMA MOJA
Moja looks at Oya like, "What I say?"
What I say?

OYA

Mama I . . . You . . .
What you mean?

MAMA MOJA

A mother's stare . . .

OYA

Mama please!

MAMA MOJA

I'm tired of you coming in here
All skin't up from running.
Running got your body all hurt.

OYA

I ain't hurt. I'm fine.
I just . . . I have to run today.

MAMA MOJA

You must not be too good
You come in here all breathin
Hard, dirty and funky and all,
Ankles all swollen. You a good
Runner?

OYA

Yes Mama.

MAMA MOJA

You sure?

OYA

Yeah I'm sure!

MAMA MOJA

Oh yeah? That's what they say, huh?

OYA

That's right. I know you heard.
I'm Oya.

MAMA MOJA

Laughing! UH-HUH!
I know that's right!
Now that's what I wanna hear!
You gon out there and show them
Girls how to.

OYA

Oya laughs at her crazy mama.
You crazy.

MAMA MOJA

You my favorite Oya Jean Fair.

OYA

I'm your only Mama Moja.

MAMA MOJA

I know that.
Trying to see if you know.
Let me look at you.

OYA

Here I go.

MAMA MOJA

They stand for each other.
A reflection . . .

OYA

A face.

MAMA MOJA AND OYA

Her own.

MAMA MOJA

(Sharp breath)
Ah!
Moja's breath comes loose.
She catches her knee.

OYA

You okay Mama?

MAMA MOJA

Gon head to your meet.
Gon head. I be here when you
Get back. Tired just now.

OYA

You sure Mama?

MAMA MOJA

Gon. I don't want you missing this one.
Gon.

OYA

All right.
Oya leaves.

MAMA MOJA

To run her race.

ELEGBA

Enter Lil Legba
Moja!

SCENE 2

MAMA MOJA

Not today Lord . . .

ELEGBA

Moja!

MAMA MOJA

Loud as hell . . .

ELEGBA

MA MOJA!

MAMA MOJA

Moja steps to the porch.

ELEGBA

MA . . .

MAMA MOJA

Lil Legba! What I told you bout hollarin fa me huh?
Screamin my name like that!

ELEGBA

Sorry Moja.
Where Oya?

MAMA MOJA

Runnin . . .

ELEGBA

Already . . .

MAMA MOJA

Always.

ELEGBA

I come to beg some candy or some money to get some.

MAMA MOJA

No.

ELEGBA

I know it's bad for me, I know it but Mama Moja
I have to have it, I need it in my life!

MAMA MOJA

Moja looks at him like, "What I say?"
What I say!

ELEGBA

What I got to do to prove to you I need it?

MAMA MOJA

You don't need it.

ELEGBA

What I got to do to prove I gots to have it?

MAMA MOJA

You can whatever you please,
Telling me what you gots to have,
I ought to spank your tail!
Send you round back to your peoples
So they find out you round here begging.

ELEGBA

They don't mind you giving, Mama Moja,
Sweet Moja. They know you. We love you.

MAMA MOJA

Moja smiles.
You ain't getting no candy Legba.

ELEGBA

Damn.

MAMA MOJA

What you say?

ELEGBA

Somebody say you know dreams.
You understand dreams Mama Moja?

MAMA MOJA

I mayhap.

ELEGBA

Sometimes I come home from the schoolhouse tired . . .

MAMA MOJA

Uh, Lil Legba . . .

ELEGBA

Fall asleep . . .
I dream with messages I can't read yet . . .
Need some help with.
I know they messages, just don't know who they to,
Where they from, how to get them there.

MAMA MOJA

Moja sighs. Giving into the lil fucker . . .
What your dreams say Lil Legba?

ELEGBA

I don't know that's what I'm asking you.

MAMA MOJA

Go on Lil Legba . . .

ELEGBA

They hurt now these dreams . . .

MAMA MOJA

Tell me your dreams lil boy!
Mumbling to herself,
Shitc'monIain'tgotalldayforthisfoolishness.
Sorry Lord.

ELEGBA

It's always about the water, my dreams.
Near it or around it. Sometimes I stand
In the high tide and I can't breathe but I
Can breathe. And I walk on the bottom on
The floor of the waters and they's these people
Walk alongside me but they all bones and they

Click the bone people, they talk in the click.
I say, "Where yall going?" And they say, "Just
Walking for a while." I say, "Don't you want
To go home . . ." They say, "When we walk there, it
Wasn't there no more." I feel bad for them . . .
Then they click and I come up on the mud part,
Like they send me to the land part, And I'm
Sitting there waiting 'cause I know they want
Me to wait I wait there looking and on
Top of the waters is Oya . . .
Lil Legba looks for Moja's reaction.

MAMA MOJA

ELEGBA
Oya girl floating on top of the water,
Looking up towards the sky and with no clothes
She hardly got no clothes on and she got her legs
Wide . . .
Lil Legba ducks . . .

MAMA MOJA

ELEGBA
And she holding her head on the side with her
Hand like something ailing her.
But from her legs blood coming down and it's making the
    pond
Red . . .
All the water around her red but she
Ain't in pain Mama Moja she ain't in
No pain it look like just laying on top of
That water. Brown skin in the red water

And I stick my hand in the water to make
It wavy so she see me on the land I want
To ask her something but she don't look
At me so I stick my hand in the water to make
It shake her on top and the water comes back in
A wave, that red and brown water, wash on me
And I wake up sweating on my face and wet
Low down, like that water, between my legs, wet . . .

MAMA MOJA

Mama Moja moves to slap his lil fresh face.

ELEGBA

UHUHYOUTOLDMETOTELLYOU!

MAMA MOJA

Moja standing, can't help rehearing
All that Lil Legba said . . .
Gon, Legba, watch Oya run for me.

ELEGBA

What it mean Moja?
What my dream mean?

MAMA MOJA

Mama Moja looks to the sky.
It mean you becoming a man Lil Legba,
My Oya a woman and I'm . . .
I'm tired just now.

ELEGBA

Lil Legba begins to walk away like the half moon
In the morning.

SCENE 3

The men begin chanting:

EGUNGUN
RUN!

    O LI ROON
    RUN!

        SHANGO
        RUN

            OGUN SIZE
            RUN

EGUNGUN
RUN

    O LI ROON
    RUN

        SHANGO
        RUN

EGUNGUN
RUN

    O LI ROON
    RUN

        SHANGO
        RUN

            OGUN SIZE
            RUN
            (Sharp breath out)
            AH!

(They continue.)

        NIA

Look at her!

SHUN

Running

AUNT ELEGUA

Gon head Oya!

SHUN

Running

NIA

Her powerful legs . . .

SHUN

Running

AUNT ELEGUA

Pressing that ground!

NIA

Burning it up!

AUNT ELEGUA

Yes she is . . .

NIA AND AUNT ELEGUA

Yea she is!

SHUN

Running

NIA

Faster!

AUNT ELEGUA

Then faster!

NIA

You can barely see where her feet meet the earth.

AUNT ELEGUA

Uh uh barely see where they meet.

NIA

Gon around that track!

SHUN

Running

NIA

Just love to watch her.

SHUN

Huh
Running like that.

AUNT ELEGUA

Gon head girl!

(The men stop chanting.)

ALL WOMEN

She won!

ALL

YEAH!

NIA

They all go forward to hug and congratulate.

THE MAN FROM STATE

When The Man from State cuts in front of everyone.
Oya girl you are blessed . . . Did you see how them
Other girls couldn't even keep up with you? They just
Stop running after while and just look at your
Legs flying around, flying through the air.
The white man lifts his hat so you could see his eyes,
Oya gal you got a mean run on you.

OYA

Thank you.
Kind of you.

THE MAN FROM STATE

Oya gal you come run for me like that? We
Love to have you at State, love for you to
Bring in us some championships, I ain't
Gon lie to you Oya gal we ain't got
Much in the way of offerin but you
Come be one in our school, come be one of
Our number as it were and we treat you
Right . . . we treat you good.

OYA

I . . . on't know sir I
Wish I could answer now but I gotta
Talk to my mama.

THE MAN FROM STATE

Well tell her what I said.
See what she say. Get back to me . . .
But come on quick Oya gal. That spot in
The sun ain't shining eternal.

OYA

Oya breathes and smiles.

OGUN SIZE

That beautiful smile.

SHANGO

But she was bleeding.

ELEGBA

Everyone saw it.

OGUN SIZE

How could they not?

OYA

Oh I . . .

*(The men all step toward Oya.
The women block them out.)*

OYA

I . . . I just . . .

SHUN

Didn't you know it was coming?

OYA

Well I . . . I mean . . . 'cause of the running . . .
It gets off and . . .

SHUN

Huh.

NIA

She didn't know.

AUNT ELEGUA

Oya . . .

SHUN

Stupid girl.

SCENE 4

OGUN SIZE

Ogun Size on Oya's front porch.
F F Fine runnin out there.

OYA

Hey Ogun, how you doin?

OGUN SIZE

So, so beautiful . . .
I mean to, to see you . . .
I mean to, to see you run like that
So beautiful.
Make me almost wanna fall asleep.

OYA

OGUN SIZE

I mean, not 'cause I'm . . . No because you, it's
It's, it's got this song to it your legs like
A crickets, but more beautiful but still when
They . . .

Ogun moves his fingers like legs runnin,
When they move *like* this they start stir, stirring
A song in the air . . . like, like a lil lullaby . . .
Sing-singing to me softly. Move so so
Fast they start to sing. You know?
In the a-air, O-Oya in the air.

OYA

Oya sad, smiles.

OGUN SIZE

What's wrong?

OYA

You hurt my heart. When you stutter like that.

OGUN SIZE

I . . . I do that! I don't . . .
Giving effort to not stutter,
Mean it Oya.

OYA

I know. It's like I know you . . . What you want to say and
sometimes when it halts up like that when the words get
stuck in your chest, when they could come out so sweet
I just . . . I get sad for you . . . that's all.

OGUN SIZE

Oya I . . . I . . . I . . .

SHANGO

Enter Shango.
What up, Ogun?

OGUN SIZE

He-Hey . . .

SHANGO

C'mon nigga get it out.

OGUN SIZE

I . . . Hey Shango.

SHANGO

How you doin man?
I see you trying to woo the ladies
Still which yo half-out words.

OGUN SIZE

Oh man stop, stop teasing me.

SHANGO

Nah I ain't teasing you man . . .
You my man Ogun.

OGUN SIZE

Hey Shango . . .

SHANGO

You think I can talk to Oya here for
A minute?

OGUN SIZE

Oh . . . uh . . .

SHANGO

Shango steps in front of Ogun.
Thanks man I preciate it.

OGUN SIZE

Ogun leaves the way he came.

SHANGO

Oya gal, Oya gal.
You ran that race.

OYA

How you doin Shango?

SHANGO

Oh I'm phyne . . .
You know
Shango laughs
I'm fine.

OYA

That's good.

SHANGO

You looked so good out there, girl. So good.
Running
Yeah you was.
Till you started bleeding but still . . .
You know you can't help that.
Nah. But still damn.
He adjusts his dick.
He puts his leg up.
He licks his lips.
I rarely look at dark girls like that,
But you black and phyne.
So I couldn't help it.

OYA

Huh.

SHANGO

Nah don't get all like that.
Why dark women always
Got to get mad so quick?

OYA

We can't change color, like the yellow girls when they blush
So we get mad quick so you can see it in our face.

SHANGO

You crazy girl. Why you so crazy?
You smell good. Oya how you been running all
Day and still smell good.

MAMA MOJA

(Offstage)
'Cause I teach her to wash every day.
Enter Mama Moja.
And not to play with trash . . .
I say Oya gal . . .
Moja moves in.
Don't play with trash, hear,
It gets in yah eyes, baby,
It gets in yah eyes.

SHANGO

Oh how you doin Ms. Moja.

MAMA MOJA

Evening come Shango.
Yo mama missing her third born.

When the rent time come she don't pay
No portion of it for over here . . .
Think you need to enjoy what she pay for.
Think you need to be where she prepare a place for you.

SHANGO

You have a good night, Oya.
Exit Shango.

MAMA MOJA

Some of the nastiest things come wrapped like that . . .

OYA

He all right Mama don't mix words on him,
He just smelling himself.

MAMA MOJA

The scent strong . . . You sure you don't smell him too?

OYA

Mama!

MAMA MOJA

Boys start smelling and those that was ladies and gentleman
Something start coming away and they get back to animals
    again
Sniffin each other.

OYA

He gone Mama, Shango just silly like boys get.
Mama.

MAMA MOJA

Moja, not listening, folds a little.
Uh.

OYA

Mama!

MAMA MOJA

Moja holds out her hand and waves Oya back.
Just tired.
Take me inside please.

SCENE 5

THE MAN FROM STATE

The Man from State stands.

OYA

Oya looks out forward. Head high.
I don't know how to say this sir. Yes I
Do. First I say thank you, sir, very much I
Wish I could come on with you this year I do.
I love to run. Nobody loving kicking
Up dirt on a track like me. That I know,
That I feel. But I love my mama. And
She been low lately. Low. She say she ain't
Got long. I don't believe her but I do.
And sir you don't know but I'd be lying
If I say I wouldn't go crazy if something
Happened to Moja while I was away.
She say just a year, this year. I stay

With her this while. I will that's what I will do.
But I'll keep training keeping running, always
Running. I know there might not be a chance
Next year but there might be. But there may not be
Moja when I got back . . . So I'ma stay here. To
See her stay or . . . go. Thank you so much sir.
Have a good year.

SCENE 6

OYA

It was late one night,
Early one morning . . .
Ah!
Oya wakes from a dream.

MAMA MOJA

Moja stands in the early
Morning dew, her hair down,
Standing, staring from her porch.

OYA

Oya finds her there.

MAMA MOJA

Moja
Listening. Somewhere . . .
In the distance,

OYA

Near distance . . .

MAMA MOJA

She can hear ol death calling.

OYA

Mama.

AUNT ELEGUA

(Singing)

Gonna lay down my burdens,

MAMA MOJA

Moja throws her hand at Oya.

AUNT ELEGUA

(Singing)

Down by the riverside

OYA

Telling her to stay back.

AUNT ELEGUA

(Singing)

Down by the riverside

MAMA MOJA

Stay back.

AUNT ELEGUA

(Singing)

Down by the riverside.

                            MAMA MOJA

Mama Moja moves
To lay her cross down.

                              OYA

Oya sees it.

                            MAMA MOJA

How could she not?

                              OYA

Mama?
You hear me calling to you.
Listen to me. Like the wind calling you, Mama.

*(Mama Moja begins walking a path led by Aunt Elegua.
Oya tries to follow.)*

                              OYA

Mama!
Where you going?!

                            MAMA MOJA

Oya, in the air . . . Oya.
Go on back Oya.
This between me and the Lord.
Gon back. You can't follow.

                              OYA

But you can stay . . . Hear Mama?
I can't follow but you can stay
You know that now. Stay Mama Moja.

                              MAMA MOJA

Not now, no.

                         OYA AND MAMA MOJA

Not now.

                              MAMA MOJA

Gon head to run your race.

                              AUNT ELEGUA

(Singing)

    I ain't gonna study war no more
    Ain't gonna study war no more

                        SHUN AND AUNT ELEGUA

(Singing)

    I ain't gonna study war no more
    I ain't gonna study war no more
    Ain't gonna study war no more.

                                 OYA

And with tears in her eyes.

                              MAMA MOJA

Tremors in her body.

                                 OYA

Oya watches her mother . . .

                              MAMA MOJA

Leave this world.

(Aunt Elegua waves her hand.
Mama Moja lets out a sharp breath.)

MAMA MOJA

Ah!

(She collapses.)

OYA

Oya begins to
Weep for her mother.

ELEGBA

Enter Lil Legba, weeping!

SCENE 7

OYA

Oh Lord!

ELEGBA

It ain't right, it ain't right!

OYA

Why is he so loud?
Legba what's wrong?

ELEGBA

Yo mama's dead!

41

OYA

Lil Legba it's okay. I know . . .
Trying to comfort him and herself . . .
She ain't in no more pain!

ELEGBA

What make you think I'm crying for her?

OYA

You say . . . I say Lil Legba why you . . .

ELEGBA

Nah you didn't you say, "Lil Legba what's wrong . . . "
I tell you. I say, "Yo mama dead," that's what wrong with me.
I ain't crying for Moja what my tears do for her.

OYA

Not wanting to deal.
All right now, look.

ELEGBA

Eh I am in grief damnit!
Thinking.
You wanna grief with me?

OYA

No Lil Legba . . .

ELEGBA

What you too good to grief and wail with me?
C'mon woe the while.

OYA

Lil boy!

ELEGBA

Legba, my name Legba . . .

OYA

I know who you . . .

ELEGBA

Legba cries.

OYA

Lil Legba!

ELEGBA

Oh it ain't right this world sometimes!

OYA

No . . . No it isn't.

ELEGBA

Dead Mama Moja, dead. Who will give me lil candies
When I come by and say hi?

OYA

Legba c'mon now. I will give you . . .

ELEGBA

Legba stops crying.
Look now . . . I am griefin and moanin, all right?
Go on in the house if you gon do all that talking.
Some people ain't got no respect . . .
Legba moans.

SHANGO

Enter Shango
Hey Oya girl . . .

OYA

Shango.

SHANGO

I'm sorry bout her passin.

OYA

Thank you.

SHANGO

That always sound funny to me . . .
Somebody die and you say sorry and they say thank you
Never sound right to me.

OYA

It don't sound right to me either.
You got something more clever for me to say?

SHANGO

Nah I ain't accusing you of nothing . . .
I said it too when my daddy died
But it never felt right you know?
Never felt right.

OYA

Oya girl looks to the sky.
Finds no answer there.

SHANGO

She breathes like the wind.

ELEGBA

Legba sneaks off opposite of how he come.

SHANGO

You look like you stand some company.

OYA

Lil Legba here is . . .

SHANGO

Lil Legba?

OYA

Nothing.

SHANGO

I know I been . . .
In the past I ain't been right . . .

OYA

You got to be you.

SHANGO

That's what I say. Always be you, and . . .
People fit together different.
I fit with you different than I fit with other people
I got something drawing to you and I feel you drawing to me.
Shango curls his fingers around Oya's ear and Caresses the
    soft.

OYA

Huh.

SHANGO

So I'm lying? You don't feel nothing for me?

OYA

I ain't say all that.

SHANGO

But then . . . I mean it ain't love . . .
'Cause if it was love it would easily turn
Hate how much I get on your nerves.

OYA

That you do.

SHANGO

You get on my nerves too.

OYA

Huh.

SHANGO

But I think I adore you.

OYA

Oya takes a breath . . .

SHANGO

Tasting Shango's drift.
I like you getting on my nerves
Sometimes.

OYA

Sometimes.

SHANGO

I'm all right with that.
I like you most of the time . . .
Cept you be acting all dark-skinned.

OYA

See . . .
Niggas.
You was doing good.

SHANGO

I'm still here, I still doing all right.

OYA

'Cause my mama ain't here to run you off.

SHANGO

You know that ain't right. You know she always here.
And even if she ain't here, she there.
Shango points to Oya's heart.
And here too . . .
He points to his own.

OYA

Oya breathes.

SHANGO

Like the wind.
Let me take you inside.

OYA

I don't . . . don't need you to do that.

SHANGO

I didn't say I got to take you inside I asked to let me . . .
Shango offers his hand.

OYA

Oya sees it.

SHANGO

How could she not?

OYA

They go in . . .

SHANGO AND OYA

Together.

SCENE 8

SHANGO

WHAT!

OYA

YOU HEARD ME!

SHANGO AND OYA

SHANGO AND OYA!

OYA

FROM INSIDE!

SHANGO

YELLING SO LOUD!

SHUN

THIS EARLY IN THE MORNING!

NIA

OKAY, WAKING UP ALL THE PROJECTS!

SHANGO

Damnit Oya!

OYA

Don't cuss me in my house . . .

SHANGO

Eh fuck yo house . . .
It's too early for all this.

OYA

Why did you bring it then?

SHANGO

I ain't start this thunder!
I ain't even get up with the devil this morning!
I just said don't be all hugged up on me.

OYA

This is my house, you sleeping in my bed, next to me!
If I can't be all up on you in my house in my bed
Where I can do it then, show me!

SHANGO

I done told you.
I don't want nobody all up on me
When I'm sleep . . .
That's what the fuck I said . . .
I know I ain't stutter,
That ain't what I do . . .
Shit.

OYA

Coming outside.
Niggas!

AUNT ELEGUA

Aunt Elegua coming down the street.
Oya gal . . .
Weeping.
Oya gal!
Moaning.
Yo mama dead and gone!
Come let your Aunt Ele love you.

OYA

Hey Aunt Elegua.

AUNT ELEGUA

I don't know what I am gon do!
Yo mama's dead and gone.

OYA

She been dead for months . . .

AUNT ELEGUA

Elegua stops and looks at her smart-ass
Goddaughter.
Huh.
She breaks down again.
And I still ain't figured out what to do . . .
You need someone to watch over you!

OYA

I'm fine Aunt Elegua.

AUNT ELEGUA

Me and Moja was close.

Like a sister and now that she gone

I say to myself last night I say self that girl over there

Lonely . . .

OYA

I ain't been lonely.

AUNT ELEGUA

In that house without no one to talk to . . .

OYA

I'm fine.

AUNT ELEGUA

And here I am call myself a friend to Moja and

SHANGO

Enter Shango.

AUNT ELEGUA

Who this?

OYA

Shango this Elegua.

AUNT ELEGUA

Huh.

Yousa phyne thang ain't you.

Yes sir looka here looka here.

This here your friend Oya girl?

OYA

Yes Shango is my friend.

AUNT ELEGUA

Yall lovers and friends?

OYA

Aunt Ele!

AUNT ELEGUA

Oh honey I'm just asking ain't judging
Nah nah. Just asking. I wouldn't mind if I do . . .

SHANGO

Do what?

OYA

Huh.

AUNT ELEGUA

Nah girl I was just being silly.
You sleep here Shango baby?

SHANGO

Sometimes when Oya don't make me go home . . .

OYA

Ey!

AUNT ELEGUA

Yeah girl I figured that's how you did it.

OYA

Aunt Elegua . . .

AUNT ELEGUA

Stop all that . . . umming and ahing,
Standing like you got to pee, honey.

You don't need to dance for me
I know the story, I ain't your mama
You ain't got to splain nothing to me.
So yall sweet strong on each other or
This a bitter honeysuckle yall sipping on.
Who got which in they mouth?

OYA

We just friends Aunt Ele . . .

AUNT ELEGUA

I ain't meddlin in your business.
I ain't. I got my own business to take care of
Wondering if yo mama left me anything in the house.
Something for me?

OYA

There's a box of things I know she would have wanted you
    to have.

AUNT ELEGUA

Thank you girl.
Gon head and get it,
I'll keep an eye on God's Heaven for you.

OYA

Oya exits.

AUNT ELEGUA

You ever been with a older woman?

SHANGO

Ain't none of em like that Oya.

AUNT ELEGUA

You stepping out on my godbaby!

SHANGO

She kicks me out.
Sometimes we can't stand the sight of each other . . .

AUNT ELEGUA

But when you make up . . .

SHANGO

It's all in the making up.

AUNT ELEGUA

How she like you to make up to her?

SHANGO

Like all women do . . .
On my knees.

OYA

Oya returns.

AUNT ELEGUA

What you doing now, Oya,
With this freak here?
This boy got a wickedness in his
Stance, a driving in his pants
What a good girl doing with somebody like him . . .

OYA

I ask the same question.

AUNT ELEGUA

You ain't trying to get my baby pregnant is you.

SHANGO

Hell nah! You crazy?

OYA

Hell nah? Why you actin like that?

SHANGO

I ain't trying to have no youngin makin me grown . . .

AUNT ELEGUA

What you care? You trying to get pregnant?
Eh you can't run pregnant Oya.
You still running that man say come on in
A year . . . You ready?

OYA

Yeah Aunt Elegua, I'm running.

SHANGO

To Oya,
Lying.

AUNT ELEGUA

Don't you think it's bout time to show him you still got it
Fall coming ain't it . . .

OYA

It's just spring.

AUNT ELEGUA

You giving me mouth Oya gal,
It ain't saying what it should!
You better listen Ele when she talk yeah!
You better come on now.
Get your nose out that boy and what?

> OYA

Get your mind right.

> AUNT ELEGUA

There it is. I know you ain't forgot.
Get your books when?

> OYA

First.

> AUNT ELEGUA

Get some dick when?

> OYA

Later.

> AUNT ELEGUA

That's right be fast in the feet and not in the ass
C'mon on now. Listen to Ele.
Call up that man get him to see you can
Run like Oya gal so he can step you up.
This asphalt still be burning hot when you get back.

> SHANGO

You know that huh?

> AUNT ELEGUA

If it ain't one black road work it's another.

> OYA

Oya smiles.

> ELEGBA

A Lil older Legba enters
Breathing hard laughing breathing.

SCENE 9

SHANGO

Exit Shango.

O LI ROON

O Li Roon enters mad as hell.
Yall better get him, hear!
Catch him before I do! Because if I lay hands
On E-legba . . . I swear fore God!

OYA

What you rushing over here screaming for O Li Roon?

O LI ROON

Didn't I tell you, didn't I tell you, if you stole from me
Again Legba I was gon burn you, do something to you
Like they do 'cross the waters, in Kwait burn your booty
    hair something
So you know damnit why don't you learn? So hard-headed!
COME HERE!

ELEGBA

Legba laughing.
Running ducking.
Get off me!

OYA

What you stealin for Legba!

ELEGBA

Went in his store told him I want some candy.
He say, "Gon and get the chocolate Legba it's right there."

OYA

So you took it?

ELEGBA

I say, "I ain't got no money nah."

O LI ROON

And I say, "Then you don't want no chocolate!"

ELEGBA

And I say, "That's a bold-faced lie bitch!"

OYA

Legba!

ELEGBA

I still want chocolate whether I got the money for it
Or not . . . I still want it. He gon talk bout . . .
Nigga tell him what you said you standing right there!

O LI ROON

Let me catch hold of him,
I won't turn him loose!
Lord swear!

OYA

O Li Roon don't argue with that boy.

O LI ROON

You know that ain't no boy
This lil motherfucker been here before!

ELEGBA

You the stupidest white man I done seen!
How I been here before and I'm standing in front of you!

If I been here, you been here too
And you ought to be smart enough to know better than to
    test me!

O LI ROON

I ain't test you,
I say, "Lil Legba you don't want that
Candy man unless you got the money for it."

ELEGBA

And I shook for you.
Hell I stood on my hands to show
You . . . Emptied my pockets out and out onto the floor,
Let the lil balls of inside pocket fall out to
Demonstrate for yo half-cocked-eye ass
That I ain't had the money and wasn't gon get it soon
But that I was still salivating for that candy.
How you gon tell me what I want and don't want?
I can't stand fo nobody to tell me what I feel ain't
Really there . . . I said, "How much you wanna bet I want
    that candy!"

O LI ROON

And I got wise to that shit
'Cause the last time you brought your black ass in my store.

AUNT ELEGUA

Hold on Li . . .

O LI ROON

Oh what he ain't black?
What yall catching breath 'cause I called him what he is
I was raised here too. Right on the Bayou.
Yo mama's beat my ass with you when you got in trouble . . .

His ass is black and mine is white
His lying black ass talking about some, "I betcha a dollar I
    want that candy."
I say, "I ain't betting."
'Cause last time he took the candy and ate it through the
    wrapper, like he crazy.
Talking bout, "See there, see how much I want it. That
    prove it. I eat it through the wrapper. Just like eating
    pussy. I eat it through the panties to get it."

OYA

Oya trying not to laugh
You so nasty.

ELEGBA

Legba licks his lips.

O LI ROON

I made his lil ass get out my store talking like that nasty.
That time I just made him leave the store. But here Legba
again in my face talking about some candy. You the candy-
talkingness punk I know! I said, "Go get the money for it."
Here he go, "Oh okay," looking like a motherless child.
Long-ass arms swinging sad like a sweet chariot. I started
to give him the candy but then he gon snatch the goodie
and run.

OYA

You left to run after fifty cents worth a candy?
You got a whole store full of merchandise.

AUNT ELEGUA

And got a handful of hoodlums outside it.

OYA

You locked the door behind you Li?

ELEGBA

Hell nah . . .

AUNT ELEGUA

You gon be missing more than fifty cent
You come back honey.

OYA

Here go your fifty cent Li go back to the store . . .

O LI ROON

You so sweet, so sweet. Looking after *this* Mischief,
Caring for people around you. So good
To Everybody Oya. Remember you
Remember you watch my daughter, my
Baby girl you remember?

OYA

Yeah Li I do.

O LI ROON

She remember you Oya. You only watch her
One time but she always say to me, "Pa
Li Roon when Ms. Mama Oya come watch
Me again?" You believe that? She call you Ms.
Mama Oya!

OYA

Huh.
Oya smiles.
Huh.

ELEGBA

You still owe me fifty cent.

O LI ROON

Oh I got the whole G-unit for you.
Li Roon jumps to get Legba.

OYA

Gon Li.

O LI ROON

O Li Roon exits.

AUNT ELEGUA

Who lil boy this is?

'

ELEGBA

Who big woman you is?

AUNT ELEGUA

All right now you got slick with the white man
I beat the snot out your ass and tell yo mama!
Elegua smiles.
I like him! He full of something. Like light . . .
You got pretty eyes boy. Who you leading
With them eyes? You gon be my husband
When you get grown. I promise you.

ELEGBA

You e'er break promises?

AUNT ELEGUA

Nope.

ELEGBA

I ain't neva growing up,
Yall be on suicide watch tomorrow.

AUNT ELEGUA

Oh he full of it . . .
Just life and mischief.
Sing us a song.

ELEGBA

This ain't no show!

AUNT ELEGUA

Oh nigga shut up and sing.
Shit you sit round here with all that mouth
Now somebody tell you to open it
And you shy between the teeth?
Get you ass over here sing for Aunt Ele . . .
Where did Darkness go?

OYA

Oh, he's gone like he do.

AUNT ELEGUA

Aw girl, don't worry make him miss something . . .
Go head, sing.

OYA

Yeah Legba, sing.

AUNT ELEGUA

What your name again baby?

ELEGBA

Mumblingsothatthefatladycan'thearme.

AUNT ELEGUA

Mouth!
That's what I'ma call you
Mouth.
Sing us song, Mouth!

ELEGBA

Legba smiles.
(Singing)

Lord she big
Lord see that!
Lord this lady, all woman
Born with her own rack of fat back
Lord she . . .

AUNT ELEGUA

Elegua is not amused.
You funny baby. But I know your mama,
Who e'er she is would love for my fat ass to roll
Round there and say what?

ELEGBA

Mouth was stealing?

AUNT ELEGUA

I bet you she would have a song for you.
You better find some medley in all that mouth.

ELEGBA

I got a dream I could sing.

OYA

Dream?

AUNT ELEGUA

Excited!
C'mon Mouth woo me boy!

ELEGBA

A spell comes o'er Legba.
(Singing)

Hear Legba sing
Sing of her road
Hear Legba cry
Knowing her load.

Come down peace,
Come down night
Cover over Oya girl
Make her world all right.

AUNT ELEGUA

Ah hell nigga I thought
You was gon busta rhyme
Or something . . .

ELEGBA

Legba stares at Elegua.

AUNT ELEGUA

Gon head sing yo lil song.
Everybody wanna be an idol . . .

OYA

Oya's breath.

ELEGBA

(Singing)

> She bleeds now,
> Her wounds all close,
> She breathes still
> But her chest never rose.
>
> Come down peace
> Come down night
> Cover over Oya girl
> Make her world all right.

(He hums.)

SCENE 10

THE MAN FROM STATE

The Man from State stands . . .
Oya girl . . .

OYA

Yes sir.

THE MAN FROM STATE

I am sorry Oya gal I really am I
Wished you would have come on when
I asked you to, I do. But you know
That's a good lesson on this life you

Never can tell what will happen to your
Chances you gotta jump when you can
Move, when you can move, you . . .
Young people like . . . like yourself don't have much
In the way of opportunity in this world . . .

OYA

Wait sir please . . .

THE MAN FROM STATE

I mean I would give you a chance I would
But the top girl we got she man oh man . . .
When you didn't come to us Oya gal
We had to get a second best; go there on
Our list. I don't like second nothing but such
Is life, like I told you chance to go, go, you know.
She found she was the second on our list, ooh wee.
Hell I didn't mince no words bout it I told her square
I say, "You our second. Gotta girl named Oya run
Like the wind. She say she coming on in a year."

OYA

Sir . . .

THE MAN FROM STATE

That girl found out she was our second, Oya and you would
Be surprised what people do to get to th' top some.
This here girl said to herself, I reckon, she show us good
    and plenty.
That we wouldn't wanna look nowhere else when we
See what she can do. Took about seven off her time . . .
Just like that. Every time since she stepped on our grassy?
She been running for her life look like.

Seven consistent. Seven like that . . . and then more.
I never seen nothing like it in m'life.
Never.
I do hope you keep training there Oya.
And you know keep yourself up . . .
But we just ain't got no place for you here.
No, not here.

OYA

Oya sad, smiles.
Taking it in.

(Elegba hums.)

SCENE 11

SHANGO

Enter Shango, dressed in an Army Recruit uniform.

(Elegba hums.)

OYA

What you come to tell me dressed like that?
We . . . we through? That's what you saying?

SHANGO

OYA

Nothing to say? Huh.
All the years I know'd you got mouth to say
What come to it now what? Speechless?

(Elegba hums.)

OYA

Shango just speak your words and I'll be free.
Free from you coming, tasting me at night,
Me smelling you smelling like somebody else
Yeah say it, un spell me Shango. Do me a favor.
That's what you gon say right? That's what you doing me
    a . . .

SHANGO

Shango moves to . . .

OYA

No!

SHANGO

OYA

I ain't going to school no more . . .
I, they ain't got no place for me.
Nowhere for me to go but here, I'm here.
I can't go nowhere. Just be here.
Here.

SHANGO

Shango curls his fingers around Oya's ear
And Caresses.

OYA

SHANGO

Exit Shango.

(Elegba hums.)

OYA

Oya's breath comes hard to her.

AUNT ELEGUA

They say she broke down . . .

SHUN

That's what they say.

MAMA MOJA

Or that she broke a spell.

SHUN

Broke something.

AUNT ELEGUA

Something happened.

ALL WOMEN

Something.

ELEGBA

(Singing)

> Come down peace,
> Come down night
> Cover over Oya girl
> Make her world all right.

Lil Legba exits like
A three-quarter moon in the morning.

(Oya stares out.)

SCENE 12

OGUN SIZE

Enter Ogun Size
I . . . I . . . know . . . I know that that you can he-hear me,
S So I'm I'm just standing here talking.
Standing h here speaking to you, my h heart.
Y . . . You don't know . . . You s-so blind
If you as-ask me.
I ain't n-never said nothing
Like that to you b-but how you think it make m me make me
. . . You ain't neva let me love you, but you gon lay down
And get closer to death? Snuggle up to him!
Death with his stale breath don't know you like I do.
He just a nasty ol man been looking at you since you was
Was a lil girl. But I been loving you always.
I been in love with your light and your sad eyes.
And I got this home inside me I know I do . . .
My outside seem like it's fragile but in here
A big man that will wrap you in love, Oya.
You come home with Ogun. Just come home.
You let me take care of you for a while.
I'll make it all right. I'll make it okay.

OYA

Oya stops her staring and looks at him.
You're not stuttering.

OGUN SIZE

What?
Laughing.

OYA

You not stuttering.

71

OGUN SIZE

How you feeling?
I should c-call somebody . . .

OYA

No!
Don't start again.
Don't start stuttering just talk to me.

OGUN SIZE

For the rest of my life.

OYA

OGUN SIZE

I won't skip another word. Another breath
Won't interrupt myself, you let me talk to you.
Oya in the air, Oya.
Let's go inside. We can talk quiet in there.
Come inside with me. We talk about starting
Something. Making a family one day . . .

OYA

Oya smiles.

(*The cast hums the opening.*
Ogun and Oya join them in the pantheon upstage.
Lights out.)

ACT 2

SCENE 1

Lights.
Shun and Nia dance downstage.
Oya sits on her porch.
Music plays.

SHUN AND NIA

(Singing)

> Ah!
> Ah!
> Ah!

SHUN

A Party nearby!

NIA

Going loud!

SHUN

Music!

NIA

Dancing!

SHUN AND NIA

A baby shower!
Ah!
(Singing)

    Hey!

OYA

Oya sitting on her porch,
Staring at the shower.
Look at Sophie dancing like that.
Look how big her belly is . . .
Lord.
Oya staring.
She must be so happy.

(The music changes.)

NIA

Ooh Girl!

SHUN

This is my song!

OYA

Oya on her porch.
I hate this song.

OGUN SIZE

Ogun Size enters ready for work.

This a nice song.

Better than all that noise they've been playing all night.

OYA

It's too early to go to the car shop.

OGUN SIZE

The early bird catches the worm.

OYA

OGUN SIZE

Oya, don't sit here all night and morning.

OYA

I shouldn't let you walk out there

Make you go lay down.

So I can come in later listen to you snore.

OGUN SIZE

I don't snore.

OYA

You breathe hard.

OGUN SIZE

I breathe hard . . .

OYA

OGUN SIZE

You so sweet.

OYA

Gon Ogun.

OGUN SIZE

So sweet but you can't taste your sugar.
Ogun kiss.
I gotta go, gotta go.
Ogun kiss.
See you later.
Ogun kiss.
Bye baby.
Kiss.

OYA

Don't be all up on me!

OGUN SIZE

See you later baby.

OYA

Music from the shower still going . . .

OGUN SIZE

We'll play good music at your shower one day.

OYA

One day.

OGUN SIZE

OYA

OGUN SIZE

Don't sit out there all night, Oya.

OYA

 OGUN SIZE

Ogun Size exits to work.

(The music from the party stops.)

ELEGBA

Legba sneaks in like the moon.

OYA

Oya bows her head.

ELEGBA

Legba hums.

OYA

Boy . . .
Why you always sneaking?

ELEGBA

I'm not sneaking,
I'm watching.

OYA

You getting too big to be doing that.
Watching me. I know those looks . . .

ELEGBA

I can't do nothing with them.

OYA

People talk about those looks Legba.
People talk bout you Legba.

ELEGBA

So you heard?

OYA

Who ain't heard about you getting kicked out,
Your mama putting you out?

ELEGBA

I'ma man now Oya.

OYA

Don't think she ain't gon take you back . . .

ELEGBA

She say don't be back for nine months.
Don't come back till it's born.

OYA

ELEGBA

OYA

Who? You got somebody pregnant?

ELEGBA

Legba beams like the moon.

OYA

Legba how old is that girl?
She my age?

ELEGBA

She ain't no girl.
Oba all woman.

OYA

You always did like older women.
What she doing messing with you?

ELEGBA

She say I got an old soul.
I say, "I'm just sixteen."
She say, "In this lifetime but you really like fifty."
I say, "Yeah right but when I lay you down
You will know why they say boys never stop
Playing with they toys."

OYA

Boy shut up!
Laughing!
So nasty!

ELEGBA

Never stop playing with they food either.
You know I can eat. I love some chocolate too . . .
The older it get, sugar just rise to the top . . .
Slurp.

OYA

See that woman right you
A dirty old man in there.

ELEGBA

OYA

ELEGBA

I can't stop being happy about this.

OYA

I can't stop smiling at you.

ELEGBA

We wrong Oya?
It ain't right to be just bringing babies in this world . . .

OYA

What else we got to do? Nothing. Sit around
Watch the world. Babies got some sunshine in em.
I saw some little bowlegged baby
Walk round here the other day just as cute
I looked at her and I said, "Whose baby is this? . . ."
She looked at me, "Not yours . . ." She wasn't mean
She just say it matter of fact and bent down
Picked one them firecrackers left from the Fourth
I say, "Lil baby don't eat that."
She put it right in her mouth and started chewing
Like it was this brand-new flavor Now and Later
Just chewing and the burnt orange of the gunpowder
Flowing out her mouth . . . she just smiling.
Her mama walk by and grab up the baby,
"What the fuck you got in your mouth?"
Starting spanking her.
"Didn't I tell you to not put shit in your mouth . . ."
The baby start crying. She carrying the baby away looking at
Me talking bout, "And you just gon sit here and let her kill
    herself?"
I wanted to be like, "Bitch that ain't my baby
She just told me I wasn't her mama . . ."
Why she let the baby just roam around the projects
Any damn way? As much as they shoot round here?
Letting your child just walking around here. Unchecked!

ELEGBA

Legba looks at Oya girl.

OYA

Oya girl feels him staring.
Go in there and get some sleep.
Look like you been up all night.

ELEGBA

Ogun . . .

OYA

He gonc to work . . .
You need to sleep gon head . . . Daddy.

ELEGBA

Thank you Oya.

OYA

Uh-huh.

ELEGBA

Legba sneaks off like the moon behind a cloud
Gone but still there.

(Elegba hums.)

SHANGO

Enter Shango dressed in Army Fatigues . . .

OYA

Oya's breath.

SHANGO

Shango stands in a better light.

OYA

A sad song plays . . .

SHANGO

Sad like when you were little.

OYA

Sad like a mother's heartbreak.

SHANGO AND OYA

Sad . . .

SHANGO

I saw Legba go in.
What he doing here?

OYA

Minding his business . . .

SHANGO

That lil boy got business over here?

OYA

He ain't that little no more.
He about to be a daddy.

SHANGO

I been gone that long huh?

OYA

Long enough.

SHANGO

Surprised you ain't swollen up.
You with somebody I know.

OYA

If you know why you asking?

SHANGO

Who you been down together in
Your sleep with?

OYA

How all of this your business, huh?
Didn't you just get here?
Say your hellos to everybody,
They will tell you all
The news you wanna know.
I'm not your reporter, seek your
Prophecy elsewhere.

SHANGO

You ought to be swollen, belly full,
Glowing with that morning glow . . .
Titties perky ready to give life . . .

OYA

I ain't trying to have no youngins making me grown.
Remember that? Please boy. Gon, okay?
Gon Shango.

SHANGO

Shango curls his fingers . . . He Caresses . . .
You still slim and ripe . . .

How somebody ain't put
A baby inside you yet is beyond me.
Exit Shango.

SCENE 2

OYA

Oya
Laughs to herself.

AUNT ELEGUA

Aunt Ele sees it,
How could she not?
Ooh Oya gal Oya gal!
Where you coming from smiling like that?
Tell me I love women's secrets!

OYA

I just came back from . . .

AUNT ELEGUA

He home ain't he?
Shango!
He home from the war or
The crisis . . . whatever . . .
Your Fire is back!
Girl you better go get melted down!

OYA

Shhh! Aunt Ele, I'm with Ogun . . .

AUNT ELEGUA

Yeah but he don't walk near you and
Your temperature change. I have seen you.
I know what you're like under Ogun Size.
But it ain't nothing like that lightning
From Shango, eh?

OYA

Aunt Ele!

AUNT ELEGUA

Shango come and he walk over to you
Your knees clap down, you fall
On that bed, honey that muscle just
Grinding on his thigh aching to touch . . .
You start to change color you start
To lose your breath, how they say
(Singing)

Huh-huh can you keep up? . . .

OYA

Your nephew loves me . . .
I love him . . .

AUNT ELEGUA

Something bout that say "lie" to me.
I got to go, I just come thought I be nosy
Come see if you nosy.
Come see if your nose wide open.

SCENE 3

From offstage, the cast hums a gospel or spiritual.

> OYA

Sunday afternoon.
Oya sitting on her porch.

> NIA

Nia and Shun walk by.

> SHUN

Laughing to themselves.

> NIA

There go the girl, Shun, almost let Shaunta
Kill herself by eating a fireworks. Yeah!
Remember I told you.

> SHUN

Oya Jean Fair almost let my godbaby die, Nia?

> OYA

I told her not to.
She's got a grown lil mouth.

> SHUN

You should have popped her hand or something.
You grown ain't you?

> NIA

Now you know I would have come round
Here and beat Oya ass she would have hit
My baby.

SHUN

Laughing . . .

NIA

What?

SHUN

I could just see Shaunta telling
Oya, "You ain't my mama!"

NIA

Laughing too!
Yeah!
To Oya
She so bad sometimes . . .

SHUN

Ooh I love her.

OYA

If she was my baby . . .

SHUN

She ain't your baby you
Ain't got no baby.
Don't run out with your mouth.
Tend to your lil grease monkey.

NIA

Don't act like that Shun.
Nia and Shun leave.

SHUN

Laughing.

(The cast upstage hums.)

SHANGO

Enter Shango.
You weren't at church.
How long it's been since you talk to Jesus?

OYA

Don't do that.

SHANGO

I'm just concerned about your soul . . .
I wanna see you in the sky when we
All get there.

OYA

Service still going why you left?

SHANGO

Ah hell I had to get outta there.
It's going on four!
First they started late, then the choir . . .

OYA

Legba was up there?

SHANGO

I saw him . . .
Him and Ogun's brother, Oshoosi.
If I was Ogun I would ship Oshoosi ass
Off to military school . . .
Thirteen years old, getting thrown in jail.

OYA

Oya looks up.

SHANGO

Yeah, that's why the church going so long.
They praying for his monkey ass.
Choir just up there singing.
Elegua came in to the church she mad
As hell. You can tell 'cause her wig all
Tilted to the side and she walking that
Big girl walk towards the altar. She
Talk to the secretary of the mother's board, Mother Pickalo.
Whatever Elegua telling her making her shake and put
    down her head.
She starts praying. I'm like, "What the hell's going on?"
Elegua walk up to the choirstand and she just
Start to beating on Oshoosi. Beat beat beat . . .
All the way down the aisle of the church and out
The front door. Mother Pickalo, she stands up like she bout
    to declare war.
She standing there you know in the church lady stance
You know with her face fully forward Holy Ghost filled,
Double chin jangling. Gon talk about, "Giving honor to
    God, yall
I have some news, you know times is hard.
And the devil is out there I know!" People "Amen-ing" and
    "Yes Lordin."
I'm like I wish this chick would come the hell on
And stop the testimony . . . But you know she crying:
"And Lord the devil can sometimes sneak in here
Too . . . This holy sanctuary, Lordie G Lord!
This temple . . . this house of God can be sacked with
    wasteful . . .

There was money being stolen from
Out the mouth of God and being used
To play in some corner crap game
Filled with wicked youthful derision. Lord God Lord God.
I ask that this money be prayed over and
Put back into the rightful hands of the church
So it can pay for the pastor's sons' gonorrhea of the mouth!"

OYA

She didn't say that!

SHANGO

How you know you wasn't there?

OYA

Elegua came and told me she put Oshoosi in jail for a day . . .

SHANGO

So you knew this whole time, huh?
What you let me tell it for?

OYA

Wanted you to tell me something.

SHANGO

He smiles.

OYA

She smiles . . .

SHANGO AND OYA

They . . .

SHANGO

Shango curls . . . He Caresses . . .

ELEGBA

Legba sneaks in unseen. A bundle in his arms . . .

OYA

Oya smiles.

SHANGO

You tell me something,
What you doing with Ogun Size?

OYA

The same thing I was doing with you . . .

SHANGO

He doing it right?

OYA

Lying.
Every night.

SHANGO

Like me? Nah not like me.
He eat that pussy like me?

OYA

You oversteppin Shango!

SHANGO

How you mean, I was there first . . .

OGUN SIZE

Where you at now Shango?
Enter Ogun Size.

SHANGO

Shango grins . . . A glint of war in his eyes.
Hi, hi, you doing Ogun . . .

OGUN SIZE

Oh I'm phyne . . .
You know . . .
Ogun laughs in mimic of Shango.
I'm fine.

OYA

Oya interrupting
Gon Shango.

SHANGO

Smiling
I was there first . . .
I'll be there last.
Exit Shango.

OYA

OGUN SIZE

OYA

OGUN SIZE

ELEGBA

A baby cries inside.

OYA

You hear a baby crying?

OGUN SIZE

Yeah.

OYA

They move to the door . . .

OGUN SIZE

You wanna go in now?

OYA

Gon Ogun . . .

OGUN SIZE

You stay outside too much Oya.
You need stay in sometimes.
It ain't right for you to be out here all the time.
One day you'll have something to stay in for.

OYA

Let me see what's in my house.

OGUN SIZE

You should already know.
You know?
You should know already.

SCENE 4

Shun and Nia stand and hang clothes on a line.

SHUN

Hum.

NIA

Huh?

SHUN

Hum, so nobody can hear.

(Nia hums.)

SHUN

Sharing a secret.
Girl Legba mama came round to Oya house
Screaming and carrying on!

NIA

Laughing,
Back to humming.

(Nia hums.)

SHUN

Yeah girl! 'Cause Legba done
Took his baby and been hiding
Out at Oya House.

NIA

So his mama got the baby now?

SHUN

You supposed to be humming?
I'm supposed to be telling!

NIA

Nia hums.

(Nia hums.)

SHUN

So yeah Legba mama got the baby now,
And she told Legba to stay at Oya house.

(Nia hums.)

SHUN

Oya got a full house,
'Cause now Ogun ask
Elegua to stay round there!

NIA

What?

SHUN

Yeah girl!

NIA

Nia hums.

(Nia hums.)

SHUN

The night before Ogun woke up and
Saw Oya sitting on the porch rocking . . . You

Remember it was during the blackout
All the power was out in the projects.
Anybody in they right mind be inside
Not sitting on they porch but Oya
Say he don't know seem like she losing her mind
Ask Aunt Ele come and watch her.
But I know the bitch ain't crazy nah
She a lil hotbox and she been getting a visitor.

                                NIA

Who?

(Nia hums.)

                                NIA

Shango!

(Nia hums.)

                                NIA

But you knew that was coming
I know you ain't mad?

                              SHUN

What you talking bout Nia!
I ought punch you in your damn face!

                                NIA

Ah bitch you jealous you ain't crazy, huh.

                              SHUN

Huh.

NIA

Consoling her friend.
They was together before he left.

SHUN

I don't care if they was *married* before she stealing
My man now.

NIA

You know Shango ain't nobody man.

SHUN

Yet . . . You just got to learn how to tether niggas.
Just sing your song Nia.
Don't worry bout Shun okay
'Cause when it come to it . . .
I know how to run Miss Oya
Where she can't walk.

NIA

Nia smiles at her friend.
She hums.

(Nia hums.)

SCENE 5

OGUN SIZE

Why you let her go?

AUNT ELEGUA

She grown and got legs
And I asked her to go . . .

And further who you think you talking to boy?
I ain't got to splain hell of nothing to you!

OGUN SIZE

Aunt Ele I don't wanna get into it . . .

AUNT ELEGUA

But you step yo flat foot right in it!

OGUN SIZE

Oya ain't feeling good!

AUNT ELEGUA

Who you to say that girl ain't feeling good?
She a grown woman ain't she?
Grown enough to know what is and ain't.

OGUN SIZE

She sitting out, sneaking out all the time.
Staring got this look on her face.
She got a sad look on her always . . .

AUNT ELEGUA

Hell life like that . . .
You think sadness stop niggas
From going to the fish market?

OYA

Oya enters . . .

OGUN SIZE

Smiling . . .

AUNT ELEGUA

Carrying a bag.

OGUN SIZE

Let me get that for you.
Where you been?

OYA

Now wait . . . you just took the bag from me.
Where it look like I been?

OGUN SIZE

Did you leave outta here carrying that grin?
Where you pick that up from?

OYA

Oya stops smiling
Nowhere.

OGUN SIZE

I'm serious . . . I ain't seen your face like that in a long time . . .
No round me.
I just wanna see it . . . I . . .
I love it . . .
I love you.

OYA

I gotta help with the fish.

OGUN SIZE

You know I don't eat fish . . .

AUNT ELEGUA

It's Friday boy . . .
Friday the best day for some fish. I never
Did understand my sister's kids. Some of
The most finicky eaters. You won't eat fish . . .

That Oshoosi talking bout he can't have no
Banana pudding 'cause it make his throat itch.
On top of that neither one of the niggas take in
Milks without farting all over the house. Never
Understood how yall get these delicate stomachs
When you starving . . . seem like to me yo stomach
Be glad to get anything in it. C'mon stay
For some of this fish. You don't eat enough nohow.

OGUN SIZE

Should I stay Oya?

OYA

Go on in and lay down fore we eat.

OGUN SIZE

Ogun Size exits hoping to see her smile . . .
But only finds a dark cloud in Oya's sky.

OYA

Oya looks to Elegua

AUNT ELEGUA

I'll start the seasoning . . .
Aunt Elegua exits.

OYA

Oya bows her head.

ELEGBA

Legba tries to sneak in the door with the baby.

OYA

Legba yo mama say you can't keep the baby round here you
want her to come here and be mad with all of us.

ELEGBA

Legba smiles at Oya.
Oya like his sister, Oya.
He brings the baby to her.
Eh Oya look here.
He shows her . . .
Straight line of little black marks
On his leg. See?
Laughing . . .
Like the Lord was trying to send a message on it.
See it . . .

OYA

Huh . . .

ELEGBA

Hold him . . .
Legba stands back and pulls down his pants . . .

OYA

What you doin?

ELEGBA

Legba proudly shows Oya his right thigh.
Same marks. The ones like nobody ever seen
Right here on me and my baby.
You ever know something yours,
And from nowhere it proves
Itself, shows it self to be just yours only . . .
You ever felt that, Oya?
Something all yours. This mine.

OYA

Oya stares.

ELEGBA

When I hold him . . .
It's like I got more love in my hands
Than the world got air to breathe.
I don't want nothing to keep me from it.

OYA

ELEGBA

I know you understand me.
Anybody understands me you do.

OYA

Sighs.
Oya gives Legba back "more love than the world got air . . ."
Oya in the air Oya . . .
Go inside Legba.

ELEGBA

Legba fades into the house
Like the moon in the shadow of the world.

OYA

Oya breaks her spell.
That's why you named that damn baby Marc!
You fool!

ELEGBA

Legba laughs . . .
Fades into the house.

OYA

Oya smiles to herself.
Marc. Huh.

Night.
(Singing)

> Come down peace . . .
> Come down night . . .

SHANGO

Enter Shango dressed in his Army Fatigues.
Just came to say Good-bye.

OYA

All the nights I've been seeing you
And you just telling me now you leaving?

OGUN SIZE

Ogun Size enters.

SHANGO

I come to return the reins my man.

OYA

SHANGO

I gotta go.
Oya keep your head up.
I tried to leave you a lil present but . . .
I gotta go.
Ogun you stay strong man.
Keep your lil family together.
Exit Shango.

OYA

Oya curls her fingers behind her ears . . . she Caresses the soft.

(Oya hums.)

SCENE 6

OYA

Oya in the early evening
Standing on someone else's porch.
She wants to knock on the door but . . .
She hums.

(Oya hums.)

THE WOMAN WHO REMINDS YOU

Don't sing on my doorstep.
A woman of magic, a bruja,
A hoodoo-voodoo lady walks
To the porch.

OYA

I got,
My body empty . . .

THE WOMAN WHO REMINDS YOU

What you want me to do about it?

OYA

Please,
I know you know how to fix it.

THE WOMAN WHO REMINDS YOU

Go to the church ladies that's what they there
For, they all stand over you moaning and praying
They fix you right up.

OYA

They won't even see I'm in trouble.
They all say you young and you ain't pregnant?

Praise da Lord, bless
The Lord o my soul . . .

THE WOMAN WHO REMINDS YOU

God is good . . .

OYA

But He is good in all things.

THE WOMAN WHO REMINDS YOU

Huh. The Good God of a thousand and one pieces.
You looking for your piece?

OYA

You got something, some words,
That make me love right, love where I should.

THE WOMAN WHO REMINDS YOU

If you ask God of a thousand and one he will provide you
Be careful how you ask it though.
He gives you paths, none of them easy.

OYA

Then I want my own mark.
I wanna look down and see myself
Mirrored back to me.

THE WOMAN WHO REMINDS YOU

You should have had that by now.

OYA

What?

THE WOMAN WHO REMINDS YOU

You don't think by now you should have
Had something growing inside you?

OYA

No . . . No. I mean not if it wasn't time. Not if it wasn't . . .
No!

THE WOMAN WHO REMINDS YOU

But a grown woman Oya gal?
You been grown for a long time now
How you think it just skipped you?
You ain't been with no little boys.
You had how many, two grown men
From two sides of the world, the fighter
And the businessman. Both grown men
And not nar one of em filled you with seed
That growed into something? You still walking
Round here wishing for that? You should know by now . . .

OYA

What I should know?

THE WOMAN WHO REMINDS YOU

If you ain't got it in your mind I sure as shit ain't gon put it
there.

OYA

Put something here!

THE WOMAN WHO REMINDS YOU

I'ma woman, I can't put nothing there.
The hoodoo bruja goes off her porch.

(Shift.)

OYA

Oya turns. Men begin to gather.

O LI ROON

Like a rain cloud.

OGUN SIZE

You may not know . . .

SHANGO

But just like in the middle of the desert

O LI ROON

Out of nowhere comes torrential rain . . .

EGUNGUN

Around here sometimes out of nowhere . . .

ALL

A party.

SHANGO

The speakers get set up on one block . . .

OGUN SIZE

The music comes fumbling down the street

EGUNGUN

Calling you out your name.

SHANGO

It's that bass drop . . .

O LI ROON

So hard, thumping.

EGUNGUN

Dum da da, dum da da!

OGUN SIZE

It calls late, as soon as the sun downs

EGUNGUN

And again out of nowhere . . .

ALL

A crowd . . .

EGUNGUN

The Egungun assumes the position.
DJing and spinning tha hottest earth
Thumping melodies invoking sex and
Heat.
Goddamn look at the girl in the green!

SHUN

Shun . . .

NIA

And Nia.

SHUN

Walk in.

NIA

In their best public,
Yet intimate apparel.

SHUN

They walk through.

SHANGO

The men stare!

SHUN

How could they not?

EGUNGUN

Damn girl in the green came ready to ride
For real shawty what's real? Oh she acting
All stank, that's all right you be begging me
To be your baby daddy later girl.

SHUN

You better watch you mouth boi!

EGUNGUN

Aight lil mama I ain't trying to fight
Not tonight it's too thick and tight
Out here. Yall ready for that next
One? He plays a song with ride
In its rhythm, making you wanna grind where
You are.
That's it yall get to that spot
Where it's real hot. I'ma keep
Turning the temperature up
Yall just keep riding out
Specially you lil red in the green
You thick as fuck!

OYA

Oya hears that beat!

SHUN

How could she not?

OYA

She stands and watches.

EGUNGUN

It's that time of night where
Everyone in the out over here
Needs to get to know that freak within.
You know what 'm talking, specially
For the fellas. Come on yall I got a hundred
Dollars for that freshest freak girl out there.

NIA

Teasing her friend.
Go head girl.

SHUN

You done lost your mind!

NIA

That's a hundred dollars.
They say you a freak . . .

SHUN

You do it, Nia!

NIA

Ain't nobody wanna see my stretchmarks.

SHUN

Well I can't in my condition . . .

110

EGUNGUN

A hundred dollars for that nasty girl!
The one who get up here and show us all the world.
C'mon lil mama do your thang mommy.
Get up here on this speakerbox.
We want to see the way you move.
Yall scared? Why you acting shy?
After this here next song though we gon touch the sky.

ELEGBA

Enter Legba beaming like a full moon,
Bright in all white.
He moves to Oya.

OYA

Legba . . .

ELEGBA

Oya, what you doing here?

OYA

I just came to see . . .

ELEGBA

You sure . . . just to see?

OYA

Legba where the baby?

ELEGBA

My mama got him.

EGUNGUN

Appears the Egungun.
Eh my man Legba!

ELEGBA

They pull close.

EGUNGUN

Too close to be just friends.

ELEGBA AND EGUNGUN

Just friends.

OYA

Oya sees it how could she not.

EGUNGUN

The Egungun sees Oya.
This your friend?

ELEGBA

Yeah she is.

EGUNGUN

You told her about me, your friend?
She know we friends?
She wanna be friends with us?

ELEGBA

Smiling like the light of the night.
Ask her.

EGUNGUN

How you doin . . .
Oya?

ELEGBA

Yeah.

OYA

I'm all right.

EGUNGUN

You pretty . . .
Everybody tell you that though,
I know they do.

OYA

You . . . you got any kids?

EGUNGUN

Nah, nah, not yet though.
No.

OYA

Oya moves to . . .

EGUNGUN

Don't go. Let me play this song.
I'll be back . . . for both of you.

OYA

Legba . . .

ELEGBA

He will if you wait.
We can go with him . . .
You been looking, right? You came to see.
Maybe this what you looking for . . .
Maybe this fix whats broke . . .

OYA

Oya walking back.
Turns.

AUNT ELEGUA

Running into the dancing Aunt Elegua!
UH-HUH! THAT'S MY JAM MR. DJ!
Shake that goodness hey! Like Taffy Laffy!
Work it out! That's what I mean,
Dancing a "too old to be acting this young" dance!
I just cuts it loose yall, yeah I do, I get it out!
Ooh yeah honey!

OYA

Laughing how could she not!

AUNT ELEGUA

What you gon stay here all night Oya!
Girl you betta c'mon and dance it out.
C'mon real hard so you get your system
Cleaned. Work it like this!

OYA

Oya dances like Elegua.

AUNT ELEGUA

Nah gal it's like this here.
Aunt Elegua gets down with
Her big old self backing that
Thang up! Uh-huh!
That's how you do that.

OYA

Laughing . . .
A cloud passes.
I don't feel good Aunt Ele.
You come to get me?

AUNT ELEGUA

Came to show you a way home.

SCENE 7

OYA

Oya girl sitting on the front porch
Humming and then crying. Smiling.
Then humming again.

SCENE 8

OGUN SIZE

Ogun Size enters.
Oya.

OYA

You don't need to be there.

OGUN SIZE

Oya you just hurt.

OYA

You don't know . . .

OGUN SIZE

Please let's go in . . .
I'll take care of you.

OYA

I don't need you to take care of me.

115

OGUN SIZE

Oya one day we . . .

OYA

No! No more days! None!
What you got?
You gon be stuck here like me forever.
Just us so what you got?
What I need you to do for me?
Gon head Ogun
Gon head . . .

OGUN SIZE

Ogun turns.

OYA

You was good to me . . .

OGUN SIZE

Ogun begins to turn back.

OYA

Don't turn around!
You was good to me,
And I loved you.
Go find somebody who love you better.
Don't . . . turn.
Gon head now . . .
Gon head.

OGUN SIZE

Ogun Size leaves his heart behind.

OYA

Legba enters like the moon during the day, there but not
    saying anything.
Legba, Legba, Legba!
You surprised me!

ELEGBA

OYA

I didn't know you was like that!
I didn't know you was into things like that.
I mean I know you got a lil freak in you . . .

ELEGBA

Legba smiles.

OYA

Legba.
You a gray boy?

ELEGBA

I got a son.

OYA

Gray boys have sons.

ELEGBA

I came to tell you . . .

OYA

Don't . . .
I don't feel . . .

ELEGBA

Shango is home.

OYA

Oya curls . . .

ELEGBA

He coming here I saw him.
He stopped by Ogun and shook his hand first.
Say he sorry how he acted before.
Say now that he grown . . . He need to say his sorrys.

OYA

Huh.

ELEGBA

I dream about you Oya.

OYA

Gon now Legba.

ELEGBA

It's always been the same . . .

OYA

Gon!

ELEGBA

Elegba walks away, staring at Oya.

OYA

Shun and Nia enter to give me more bad news.

SHUN

Don't . . .
No, now!

NIA

C'mon on now Shun be a good neighbor!

SHUN

Fuck that . . . Fuck that!
Under her breath:
I don't like that . . . I don't see why
I have to . . .
She crazy anyway!

NIA

Go on girl stop being like that.
To Oya:
Hey!

OYA

Hey!

SHUN

NIA

Shun!

SHUN

Ah shit!
I guess you've heard . . .

OYA

I know Shango back.

SHUN

Yeah I guess you would know that.
But you heard about me?
Me and Shango?

OYA

You and Shango what?

SHUN

You better act like you happy for me
Looking all sad n shit . . .
You better know.

OYA

Happy for what?

SHUN

Smile.

NIA

Shun got Shango's baby.

SHUN

I'm having his baby
So I'm his woman now!
You ain't shit to him.

NIA

Shun!

SHUN

Heavy breath!
But I was gon come to
Invite you to the shower we having,
Ifyoucanmakeit. See I said it les go.

OYA

Thank you . . .
I don't think I'll be there.

SHUN

Good . . .
I mean yeah . . .
Come on Nia.

OYA

Oya's breath comes loose . . .

SHUN

You all right?

OYA

Yeah I just gotta go inside
I gotta get a gift for Shango.

SHUN

Where my gift?

OYA

You already got it.

NIA

Come on Shun.

OYA

Oya with light in her eyes
Enters her house.

NIA

SHUN

OYA

Nia and Shun leave.
Shango enters.

121

SHANGO

He stands in his officer's uniform.

OYA

(Offstage)
You out there now Shango!
I know you are . . .
I be there in a minute!

SHANGO

Good to see you Oya gal.
Take your time . . .

OYA

I know you a busy man now
I heard your good news,
I heard your good news!
So I said let me get him something,
A present so he remembers me in his new life and times!

SHANGO

You didn't have to do that.

OYA

Yes I did . . .
I have to do it.

ELEGBA

Legba enters like the moon eclipsing the sun.
(Singing)

She sleep now
But her eyes still open

Yes sleep now
But her tears still flowin.

OYA

Oya enters
Holding her hand to her head.

SHANGO

Shango moves to curl his fingers.

OYA

But Oya's hand . . .

SHANGO

Holding her head . . .

OYA

Is blocking him.

ELEGBA

(Singing)

Come down peace
Come down night
Cover over Oya girl
Make her world all right.

OYA

In the other hand, her left . . .
Oya gives it to Shango.
I do this in remembrance of you . . .
I wished I could make a part of me
To give you but I had to take what's

Already there . . . Just give you what I got.
Oya bleeds, down her right hand.

ELEGBA

(Singing)

She bleeds now

SHANGO

You . . .

OYA

Open it . . .

ELEGBA

(Singing)

Her wounds all close

SHANGO

Shango opens his hand . . .

ELEGBA

(Singing)

She breathes still

OYA

Oya moves her hand from where her ear used to be . . .

ELEGBA

(Singing)

But her belly never rose

OYA

For you to remember me by . . .

(Oya collapses down.)

ELEGBA

(Singing)

> Come down peace now
> Come down night
> Cover over Oya girl
> Make her world all right.

EPILOGUE

All save Oya stand. The men hum that sweet sad hum. Oya is center stage holding her head.

AUNT ELEGUA

I don't know about all that . . .

SHUN

Me neither

NIA

No one does . . .

OYA
.

Oya . . .

MAMA MOJA

Say She cut it off . . .

AUNT ELEGUA

Say that's her mark.

SHUN

Say he left her there bleeding.

OYA

A breeze over Oya.

SHUN

Somebody called her crazy so and so . . .

AUNT ELEGUA

She wasn't crazy.

MAMA MOJA

Just sad.

ALL WOMEN

Huh.

OYA

Oya . . . Oya.

AUNT ELEGUA

Say she sitting up somewhere . . .

OYA

Oya . . .

MAMA MOJA

Staring at the ceiling

OYA

Oya girl . . .

SHUN

On her back like a lake of brown . . .

AUNT ELEGUA, MAMA MOJA AND SHUN

Staring . . .

ALL WOMEN

Huh.

MAMA MOJA

My Lord.

OYA

In the air . . . Oya.

AUNT ELEGUA

Holding her head staring at the sky
You look at her,
Aunt Elegua looks to Oya,
Look like she floating somewhere . . .

OYA

In the air . . .

SHUN

Oya Jean Fair . . .

AUNT ELEGUA

My girl Oya.

MAMA MOJA

Sweet sad Oya.

AUNT ELEGUA, MAMA MOJA AND SHUN

Beautiful girl.

(Oya lets out sharp breath.)

OYA

Ah!

(Blackout.)

END OF PLAY

THE BROTHERS SIZE

To my brothers; all

The Brothers Size has been produced as part of *The Brother/Sister Plays* in numerous productions starting in 2009 (see *In the Red and Brown Water*). *The Brothers Size* was first produced at the Yale School of Drama in 2006. It was then produced in October 2007 as part of the Under the Radar festival at The Public Theater in New York City, in association with The Foundry Theatre (Melanie Joseph, Artistic Producer). It was directed by Tea Alagic; the production design was by Tea Alagic and Zane Pihlstrom, the lighting design was by Burke Brown, the live music was by Vincent Olivieri; the stage manager was Sarah Hodges. The cast was as follows:

OGUN SIZE	Gilbert Owuor
OSHOOSI SIZE	Brian Tyree Henry
ELEGBA	Elliot Villar

The Brothers Size was produced in November 2007 at the Young Vic in London. It was directed by Bijan Sheibani; the design was by Patrick Burnier, the lighting was by Mike Gunning, the choreography was by Aline David; the music advisor was Elspeth Brooke, the company stage manager was Anthony Newton. The cast was as follows:

OGUN SIZE	Nyasha Hatendi
OSHOOSI SIZE	Obi Abili
ELEGBA	Nathaniel Martello-White

The Brothers Size was produced in November 2008 at City-Theatre Company (Tracy Brigden, Artistic Director; Greg Quinlan, Managing Director) in Pittsburg. It was directed by Robert O'Hara; the set design was by Tony Ferrieri, the costume design was by Angela M. Vesco, the lighting design was by Christian DeAngelis, the sound design was by Joe Pino; the production stage manager was Patti Kelly. The cast was as follows:

OGUN SIZE	Albert Jones
OSHOOSI SIZE	Jared McNeill
ELEGBA	Joshua Elijah Reese

CHARACTERS

OGUN HENRI SIZE	a man of color
OSHOOSI SIZE	younger brother to Ogun; a man of color
ELEGBA	best friend of Oshoosi, late twenties; of Creole heritage

TIME

Distant present

PLACE

San Pere, Louisiana, near the Bayou

A man that hath friends must show himself friendly:
and there is a friend that sticketh closer than a brother.

—PROVERBS 18, VERSE 24

PROLOGUE

The Opening Song

The lights come up on three men standing onstage. This is the opening invocation and should be repeated for as long as needed to complete the ritual.

ELEGBA, OSHOOSI SIZE AND OGUN SIZE

(Breath out!)

ELEGBA

This road is rough

OSHOOSI SIZE

Mmmm . . .

OGUN SIZE

Huh!

ELEGBA

This road is rough

OSHOOSI SIZE

Mmm . . .

OGUN SIZE

Huh!

ELEGBA

This road is rough and

OGUN SIZE

Good God!

ELEGBA

It's rough and hard

OGUN SIZE

Lord God!

ELEGBA

It's rough

OSHOOSI SIZE

Mmm . . .

OGUN SIZE

Huh!

ELEGBA

Lord God
It's rough

OSHOOSI SIZE

Mmm . . .

OGUN SIZE

Huh!

ELEGBA

This road is rough
Yeah, this road is rough.

OGUN SIZE

(Breath out!)

ACT 1

SCENE 1

OGUN SIZE

Ogun Size enters.
Osi!

OGUN SIZE

Calling for his brother.
Osi . . .
Oshoosi!

OSHOOSI SIZE

What man, what?

OGUN SIZE

Get up.

OSHOOSI SIZE

Nigga comin in here turning on lights!

OGUN SIZE

That's the sun.

OSHOOSI SIZE

Kissing his teeth

OGUN SIZE

Oshoosi!

OSHOOSI SIZE

Do you get tired of going through this?
Every morning we go through this.

OGUN SIZE

Get yo ass up!

OSHOOSI SIZE

This hard?
Early in the morning you gotta be this hard?

OGUN SIZE

Man don't bring me that . . .

OSHOOSI SIZE

That's your job.
That car shop got your name, that's your job.

OGUN SIZE

Where your job?

OSHOOSI SIZE

I ain't got none.
I am currently seeking employment.

OGUN SIZE

Currently?

OSHOOSI SIZE

I'm tired!

OGUN SIZE

So, you just gon lay up here today?

OSHOOSI SIZE

I don't sleep good at night.
Tossed and turned all this morning.

OGUN SIZE

Kisses teeth.

OSHOOSI SIZE

Man you should stay home . . .

OGUN SIZE

The shop man . . .

OSHOOSI SIZE

You own the car shop, yeah?
That car shop yours.
Say Ogun's Carshack right?

OGUN SIZE

Yeah . . .

OSHOOSI SIZE

Get somebody to work it for you.

OGUN SIZE

Deal.

OSHOOSI SIZE

What?

OGUN SIZE

You hired.

OSHOOSI SIZE

Nigga!

OGUN SIZE

You ain't got no job right . . .

OSHOOSI SIZE

You know . . .

OGUN SIZE

You "currently seeking employment . . ."

OSHOOSI SIZE

Ogun . . .

OGUN SIZE

Seek yo ass into that truck in five minutes.

OSHOOSI SIZE

Nah man, nah I'm turning this shit down.
I don't want your job.

OGUN SIZE

Wait a minute . . .

OSHOOSI SIZE

Oh shit . . .

OGUN SIZE

You turning down work?

OSHOOSI SIZE

Shit.

OGUN SIZE

Oh man you turning down a lot of shit.
First off you forfeit your living here rights . . .

OSHOOSI SIZE

Fuck that!
I'll stay with Aunt Ele!

OGUN SIZE

Gua ain't gon put up with your shit!
Elegua ain't never like us and fo sure not you.
You also forcing me to tell your parole officer
You won't work.
Smiles.
Ogun Size exits.

OSHOOSI SIZE

Are you . . .
Fo real . . .
This nigga!

OGUN SIZE

From outside
Beep.

OSHOOSI SIZE

I swear fore God . . .
I swear this nigga . . .
Got the working love, man.
Shit.
Know a nigga don't feel like no
Getting up he come in here.
"Oshoosi . . ."
Like my name slave,
Like my name on that damn car shop . . .
"Oshoosi . . ."
Nigga need to get up and build me a damn car.
A nigga need to get around.
How I'm supposed to get a girl,
Pick up, walk round on my feet?
Feet already flat.

OGUN SIZE

Beep!

OSHOOSI SIZE

You hold the hell on!
Black bastard.
If I am going to work I'ma smell G double O D good.
Can't be workin and smelling like yo ass . . .
Always funky.
Nigga stay dirty!
He ain't even that black.
I was always darker than him.
Everybody know that . . .
Damn shoe . . .

OGUN SIZE

Beep.

OSHOOSI SIZE

Keep on Og!

Keep on Ogun.

Keep on the way you do.

Every beep I'ma take even longer to get dressed.

Going in there to get oil all on me n shit.

You think I'm gon hurry up for that.

That nigga threaten to tell my parole!

He supposed to be my brother . . .

That . . .

He . . .

Boy I swear you can't win . . .

Not round here . . .

Huh!

OGUN SIZE

Coming back in.

Osi!

OSHOOSI SIZE

Eh man . . .

OGUN SIZE

Boy! Put that damn cologne down!

OSHOOSI SIZE

Look!

OGUN SIZE

Getcha ass in the car!

OSHOOSI SIZE

Laughing

Somethingtomyself'causeIdon'twantyoutohear'causeit'sforme.

OGUN SIZE

Whatcha say?
Say it again.

OSHOOSI SIZE

Mumbling man.
I don't want to hurt your feelings.

OGUN SIZE

Huh.
Ey!
Don't slam my truck . . .

OSHOOSI SIZE

Slam!

OGUN SIZE

Bastard!

SCENE 2

OSHOOSI SIZE

Oshoosi Size on lunch break,
Drinking a Coke cola
Singing a song.

(He sings.)

ELEGBA

Elegba enters . . .
Sang that song nigga!

OSHOOSI SIZE

Huh? Ey Legba!

ELEGBA

You sing nigga and the angels stop humming . . .

OSHOOSI SIZE

You crazy.

ELEGBA

It's true, brother!
Where you get a voice like that?
I been wondering since lockup,
"How Oshoosi get his voice?"

OSHOOSI SIZE

Ah hell Legba you got a voice.

ELEGBA

But my voice clear,
I know that, I was born a choirboy.
But you? You a siren.

OSHOOSI SIZE

What?

ELEGBA

A siren!
You ope up your mouth an everybody know where the pain at.
Your voice come out and say, "The pain right here.
It's here, see it? See?"

OSHOOSI SIZE

C'mon man . . .

ELEGBA

You don't like nobody to brag on you . . .

OSHOOSI SIZE

Nah man.

ELEGBA

That's all right I ain't scared to,
Everybody needs somebody to brag on him.
You like my brother man . . . I ain't scared to brag on you.
Ain't embarrassed about my brother.
Nah, too cool to be embarrassed.

OSHOOSI SIZE

My man Legba!

ELEGBA

I see Og got you round here workin.

OSHOOSI SIZE

Lookin like a grease monkey.

ELEGBA

You shouldn'ta told him.

OSHOOSI SIZE

He ask what we do in the pen.
I say, "Wait, mutha . . ."
That's what we do.
Man sometimes he ask dumb-ass questions. He ask me
    what we do in the pen.
"Wait.
Cry.
Wait."

ELEGBA

You right.

OSHOOSI SIZE

I say, "Work and wait."
He say, "Work?"
I say, "Work . . .
Cry,
Shit,
Pray nigga.
What you think?"

ELEGBA

What he say to that?

OSHOOSI SIZE

He look at me and say, "Work huh?"

ELEGBA

You shouldn'ta told him everything.

OSHOOSI SIZE

I spoke it all man.

ELEGBA

You say it all?
All about the pen?

OSHOOSI SIZE

ELEGBA

OSHOOSI SIZE

Nah I ain't tell him all that.

151

ELEGBA

Yeah that shit ain't nothin.

OSHOOSI SIZE

Nah. Hell nah.
The pen got me dreamin about pussy nightly.

ELEGBA

Man . . .

OSHOOSI SIZE

Had to hold your own self tight at night.

ELEGBA

You didn't want nobody to do it for you.

OSHOOSI SIZE

Nah. Hell nah.
Nigga's always offerin.

ELEGBA

Or trying to take it.

OSHOOSI SIZE

That shit crazy, crazy shit.
I didn't think they would get like that.

ELEGBA

Man when you in need, your mind . . .

OSHOOSI SIZE

Man . . .
Sometimes I had to remind myself,
That I wouldn't gon be there that long.

ELEGBA

Yeah you only had a year,

OSHOOSI SIZE

Two.
Man . . .

ELEGBA

We was like brothers.

OSHOOSI SIZE

Yeah.

ELEGBA

Brothers in need.

OGUN SIZE

Ogun enters covered in oil!

ELEGBA

Og!

OGUN SIZE

Niggas!

OSHOOSI SIZE

Why you got to be so hard all the time?

OGUN SIZE

You need something Legba!
I didn't see no car?

ELEGBA

Nah Og, just came to see my brother.

OGUN SIZE

Where he at?

ELEGBA

Ah, Size Number One, you know how we call each other
  brothers.

OGUN SIZE

Pissed at being called
Size Number One.
Yeah I know how.
Osi, get that part I asked you for?

ELEGBA

Well I guess I be going . . .

OSHOOSI SIZE

Take it easy Legba.

ELEGBA

Oh man you know . . .

OGUN SIZE

Yeah you be easy Legba.
Bring a car next time you come through.
Give me something to do while you brothers
Conversate . . .

ELEGBA

Converse.

OGUN SIZE

ELEGBA

Elegba exits the way he came.

OGUN SIZE

OSHOOSI SIZE

Why you always got to . . .

OGUN SIZE

I asked you for that part almost ten—

OSHOOSI SIZE

Man I took a break.

OGUN SIZE

Playin that's what you always doin.

OSHOOSI SIZE

That's my friend.

OGUN SIZE

Man you don't make no friends in the pen.

OSHOOSI SIZE

What you know?

OGUN SIZE

Bring the part Osi.

(Ogun exits.)

OSHOOSI SIZE

"Bring the part Osi."

ELEGBA

Elegba returns
Ey . . .

OSHOOSI SIZE

Oh you back man.
I gotta get to work.

ELEGBA

Nah, nah, I know.
But um listen.
You got a ride?

OSHOOSI SIZE

Nah, not yet.

ELEGBA

Your brotha the king a cars
And you ain't got no ride?

OSHOOSI SIZE

Yeah! Right.

ELEGBA

All that talk about how riding is the ultimate freedom.

OSHOOSI SIZE

I know . . .

ELEGBA

Brother you talked about cars so much,
I was scared for you to get out 'cause I swore
The first thing you was gon do was go out and steal you one.

OSHOOSI SIZE

Shut up Legba . . .

ELEGBA

I'm just saying man . . .
Remember all you talk about was a car.
I say that nigga gon get him a car.
And you ain't got no car yet.
Man please how that work?

OSHOOSI SIZE

I hear you Legba.

ELEGBA

I'm just saying man.
You know me. I don't mean nothing.
Talk too much and too slow.

OSHOOSI SIZE

Nah you all right brother.

ELEGBA

Well I will let you get back to work
I gotta get to work too.

OSHOOSI SIZE

You got a job nigga!

ELEGBA

Working at the funeral home.

OSHOOSI SIZE

Legba man you working
On dead people.

ELEGBA

Better than working with live people.

OSHOOSI SIZE

I don't like the look of the dead.

ELEGBA

You gon be dead someday too. Laying somewhere.

OSHOOSI SIZE

Yeah but I don't need yo ass to remind me.

ELEGBA

It's good to remember . . .
So you know you need to do now,
So you know that you ain't got forever just right now,
Good to remember death man.

OSHOOSI SIZE

I guess I hear you.

ELEGBA

Ey
Osi man.
I ain't mean to bring you down.

OSHOOSI SIZE

Nah man I'm all right . . .

ELEGBA

Ey see about that car Oshoosi.

OSHOOSI SIZE

Yeah yeah . . .

ELEGBA

You my brother man.

OSHOOSI SIZE

Ey man . . . I know that.

ELEGBA

Lay it down . . .
Elegba offers his hand to Oshoosi.

OSHOOSI SIZE

Oshoosi takes it, how could he not.
You all right man.

SCENE 3

OGUN SIZE

Ogun goes under the car.

OSHOOSI SIZE

Ogun . . .

OGUN SIZE

What?

OSHOOSI SIZE

I need a ca . . .

OGUN SIZE

Coming from under the car,
Holding a part, irritated.
What?

OSHOOSI SIZE

Um . . . What does that part do?

OGUN SIZE

Sighs . . . Ignoring his baby brother.
I'm trying to concentrate!
Goes back under car.

OSHOOSI SIZE

How long you think before you retire?

OGUN SIZE

I just started . . .

OSHOOSI SIZE

Yeah but shit you doing good brother.

OGUN SIZE

Huh.

OSHOOSI SIZE

Hey Og . . .

OGUN SIZE

Ogun comes from under the car.
Nigga they let you talk this much in the pen?
Ogun goes back under the car.

OSHOOSI SIZE

Oshoosi kicks at his brother.

OGUN SIZE

Ogun comes from under the car

OSHOOSI SIZE

Oshoosi smiles innocently.

OGUN SIZE

Ogun goes back under the car.

OSHOOSI SIZE

OGUN SIZE

OSHOOSI SIZE

OGUN SIZE

OSHOOSI SIZE

Man I need some pussy.

OGUN SIZE

Bang.
Shit!

OSHOOSI SIZE

And the way you running into shit you need some too.
When was the last time you had some good coochie?

OGUN SIZE

Comes from the under the car.
Coo? Did you say "coochie"?
When was the last time *you* had some?

OSHOOSI SIZE

Nigga you know the answer to that!
I ain't been out but a minute.
Shit, seen more you than I seen myself.
You know I ain't had nothing for a minute.
Man but when I do . . . Boy looka here.
BLOCKA!

161

OGUN SIZE

Looks at Oshoosi like,
"What the fuck?"

OSHOOSI SIZE

BLOCKA! BLOCKA!

OGUN SIZE

Shakes his head.

OSHOOSI SIZE

OGUN SIZE

Ogun goes back under the car.

OSHOOSI SIZE

BLOCKA!
Ey Og . . .
Og whatever happened to Oya?
Huh. That girl had a thing for you.
Man she had a thing for you.
She loved her some Ogun Size.
She was so phyne, black as night

OGUN SIZE

She was wit my boy Shango.
She stop talking to me . . . started seeing him.

OSHOOSI SIZE

Oh man I'm sorry, I didn't know, that's fucked-up . . .

OGUN SIZE

Yeah.
Yeah.

You know him right?
Go through women like draws . . . He in the Army now.
Guess he doing good.
Shango. Huh.
He say, "You should be with me.
Ogun ain't going nowhere. He ain't got no scholarship,
    nobody, no recruiter ain't looking at him . . . he just gon
    be here all his life. Be with me."
Guess it sound sweet to her.
She start seeing him, talking to him.
But he got other girls he seeing . . .
He come into town for furlough or whatever and he come
    to see em one by one.
He pay Oya some attention sometimes . . .
And then he out. He gone.
I used to see her walking around, got this sad-ass look on
    her face . . .
I wanna grab her, sometimes, when I would see her,
I wanna grab and hold her so bad.
But she ain't mine no more.
She with that nigga . . . She with him.
I . . . just respect that that's that man's girl.
She grown she in her own situation. You know . . . She . . .
Shango had this other girl . . . Guess it's his main girl.
Shun . . . She . . . man she beautiful . . . Shun. Beautiful.
All the niggas I know want her . . .

OSHOOSI SIZE

Yeah I know Shun.

OSHOOSI SIZE AND OGUN SIZE

Evil bitch . . .

                              OGUN SIZE

So she tells Oya she pregnant with Shango's baby. Just
walked up to Oya with them hips you know and was like,
"My name Shun, I got his baby so you ain't shit to him."
And see Oya can't have no kids. Everybody know that.
Something about when she was little, some accident. Now
she scared she gon lose Shango. Which would be good if
she left the nigga . . . But she can't see that, nah, she got to
show him how much she willing to do for Shango. How far
she willing to go for Shango. So she can't give him no child,
she . . . she . . .

                              OSHOOSI SIZE

What?

                              OGUN SIZE

Nothing, nothing.
Ogun goes back under the car.

SCENE 4

                              OGUN SIZE

Dinner
Unusually quiet
Eating.

                              OSHOOSI SIZE

Eating.

                              OGUN SIZE

                              OSHOOSI SIZE

OGUN SIZE

OSHOOSI SIZE

OGUN SIZE

What you up to?

OSHOOSI SIZE

Eatin my dinner . . .

OGUN SIZE

I wanna know now, Os.

OSHOOSI SIZE

Nigga?

OGUN SIZE

Tell me . . .

OSHOOSI SIZE

What's wrong wit you?

OGUN SIZE

You ain't never this quiet.

OSHOOSI SIZE

I'm hungry . . . I'm tired . . .

OGUN SIZE

Hungry?
You eatin leftovers!

OSHOOSI SIZE

Ey, I ain't ingrateful . . .

165

OGUN SIZE

That's the point you are.
You don't do nothing quiet;
You snore loud as hell,
You moan when you piss,
And when you eat you talk more
Shit than you chew!
You up to something I don't know what it is
Oshoo but you better tell me now.
'Cause if I find out you doing some—

OSHOOSI SIZE

Damn, boy I swear . . .

OGUN SIZE

I'm not gon run to your rescue . . .

OSHOOSI SIZE

Can't have no peace.

OGUN SIZE

You think, "Ogun gon get me outta this."
You can forget that shit . . .
Don't do something to put your ass back in the pen!

OSHOOSI SIZE

What?

OGUN SIZE

I said . . .

OSHOOSI SIZE

Ey man you want to go to jail Og?

'Cause you mention that shit bout every five fucking
    minutes . . .
I swear you ain't let me forget once that I, at one time, was
    not free . . .
Why you got to be so hard all the goddamn time?
Damn . . . it's gon be like this?
Let me know . . .
Let me know now 'cause I will get my shit,
Get my shit and go . . .
But while I am here . . .
Man you let me be free . . .
I got enough memories to wash out without you
Putting in a fresh supply every five minutes . . .
That shit ain't right . . .
It ain't right man . . .
It ain't.

OGUN SIZE

OSHOOSI SIZE

OGUN SIZE

OSHOOSI SIZE

OGUN SIZE

OSHOOSI SIZE

Goes back to eating.

OGUN SIZE

OSHOOSI SIZE

Eating.

OGUN SIZE

Eating.

OSHOOSI SIZE

Ey man I need a ride . . .

OGUN SIZE

I knew it!
Knew you were . . .

OSHOOSI SIZE

Nigga you the king of cars . . .

OGUN SIZE

You lookin around here?
I ain't the king of shit.
Kings don't come home greased from
The knees down.

OSHOOSI SIZE

Ey, every man's castle ain't in England man.
Every man's palace ain't made of sand
And gold and shit.
Your palace made out of them cars Og.
You put cars back together better than any nigga 'cross this
   place.
You the regent to come to about a car.

OGUN SIZE

What you need a car for?
You ain't no job to go to.

OSHOOSI SIZE

That ain't what I'm talking about.
You know what I am talking about?

You pushing the conversation somewhere else!
We talking about cars, man.
I need a ride.
I want to drive somewhere . . .

OGUN SIZE

Where?
Yo ass still on probation.

OSHOOSI SIZE

Damnit son of a bitch!

OGUN SIZE

Watch your mouth.

OSHOOSI SIZE

Damn!
I know I was once in prison.
I am out and I am on probation.
Damnit man.
I ain't trying to drive to Fort Knox?
I ain't about to scale the capitol . . .
I want a ride.
I want to drive out to the Bayou . . .
Maybe take a lady down there . . .
And relax . . .
Shit what if I just wanted to go by myself?
What if I wanted to be there alone?
What difference it make?
You can't fathom that?
You can't fit that round yo big-ass head?
You trying to lock me up again?
You trying to make my feet stuck?

Stuck here in here . . .
Well you just give me the word Og.
Tell me now like a man you want me to be miserable.
Fuck the car . . .
Mention prison again . . .
Make mention of it like you do . . .
That shit stops now.
I mean that.
I done served my time Ogun.
Sentence complete.
Done.
Done.
You sleep good tonight.
I won't.

SCENE 5

OSHOOSI SIZE

Oshoosi Size is sleeping, that night, dreaming.
And in his dream is his brother Ogun.
Oshoosi can hear him, in this dream, working,
On something, on what?

OGUN SIZE

Huh!

OSHOOSI SIZE

Oshoosi is sleeping dreaming.
Dreaming a sad dream and in his dream, enters
Elegba too. Singing a sweet song.

ELEGBA

(Singing)

Mmm-hmm.

OGUN SIZE

Huh.

ELEGBA

(Singing)

Mmm-hmm.

OGUN SIZE

Huh.

ELEGBA

Oshoosi Size.

OGUN SIZE

Huh.

ELEGBA

Cell number . . .

OGUN SIZE

Huh.

ELEGBA

Inmate number.

OGUN SIZE

Huh.

ELEGBA

Oshoosi,
Oshoosi Size.
You remember?
Don't you?
Those late nights . . .

OGUN SIZE

Huh.

ELEGBA

So hot.

OSHOOSI SIZE

So hot.

ELEGBA

When the walls come closer,
Closer . . .
At night.
Night . . .

OGUN SIZE

Huh.

ELEGBA

Deep night . . .
That's when it most dangerous . . .
'Cause sometimes in the night . . .

OSHOOSI SIZE

Night.

OGUN SIZE

Huh.

ELEGBA

You don't know what come for you, wei?

OGUN SIZE

Huh.

ELEGBA

You know not where the hand will lead you.

OGUN SIZE

Huh.

ELEGBA

If it's the good guard lead you back to your cell . . .

OGUN SIZE

Huh.

ELEGBA

If it ain't . . .

OGUN SIZE

Huh.

ELEGBA

You remember?
Me your friend . . .
Like your brother?

OGUN SIZE

Huh.

ELEGBA

I remember you . . . In there with me.
We were down in there sleep-walking together.

Got so I could tell when you wanted to eat without
You saying it . . . tell when you wanted to piss or sleep
Or . . .

OGUN SIZE

Huh.

OSHOOSI SIZE

Mmm.

ELEGBA

I know you scared . . .

OSHOOSI SIZE

Scared . . .

ELEGBA

I know you in that place.

OGUN SIZE

Huh.

ELEGBA

Prison make grown men scared of the dark again.
Put back the boogey monsters and the voodoo man
We spend our whole life trying to forget . . .

OGUN SIZE

Huh.

ELEGBA

You scared.

OSHOOSI SIZE

Scared . . .

ELEGBA

I know you are . . .

OGUN SIZE

Huh.

OSHOOSI SIZE

Dark.

ELEGBA

But I am here in the dark . . .
I come for you like I always do . . .

OGUN SIZE

Huh.

ELEGBA

In that night hour when you know nobody else
Around . . . Legba come down and sing for you . . .

OGUN SIZE

Huh.

ELEGBA

You sing with me?
(Singing)

Mmm . . .

OSHOOSI SIZE

(Singing)

Mmm . . .

ELEGBA

Yeah we sing so we know we together . . .
You and me make it so our harmony make a light . . .
In the dark.
I know you in that dark place . . .

OSHOOSI SIZE

(Singing)

Mmm

ELEGBA

(Singing)

Mmm

ELEGBA AND OSHOOSI SIZE

(Singing)

Mmm

ELEGBA

Don't cry.
Don't cry . . .
I will walk you through
Take you lightly into the night.
Make you smile.
Open your hand and smile.
That M&M kind of smile.

OSHOOSI SIZE

Hah.

ELEGBA

It's funny ain't it Osi . . .
Huh.
Funny.
Oshoosi Size . . .
My brother . . .
Can you walk with me?
I am your taker.
I am here to take you home.
Just when you thought you walked alone.
I am here.

OGUN SIZE

Osi . . .

ELEGBA

Here.

OGUN SIZE

Osi.

ELEGBA

Here.

OGUN SIZE AND ELEGBA

Osi!

SCENE 6

OSHOOSI SIZE

Oshoosi Size wakes from a nightmare
Realizing, ah hell, he late for work.

SCENE 7

OSHOOSI SIZE

Oshoosi at the shop!
Standing breathing hard
From the walk.

OGUN SIZE

Glad you could make it.

OSHOOSI SIZE

OGUN SIZE

Can you bring a box from the . . .

OSHOOSI SIZE

You left me.

OGUN SIZE

You overslept.

OSHOOSI SIZE

You wake me up every morning . . .

OGUN SIZE

You . . .

OSHOOSI SIZE

You left me there . . .
I ain't come here to work.
I quit.

OGUN SIZE

You fired.

OSHOOSI SIZE

All the better.

OGUN SIZE

You can stay.
Find a job.

OSHOOSI SIZE

I planned to.

OGUN SIZE

Then we square brother.

OSHOOSI SIZE

You left me.

OGUN SIZE

I know.

OSHOOSI SIZE

That's fucked-up.

OGUN SIZE

Huh.
You don't want me to treat you like you locked up no mo.
What you say last night Osi?
You say, "Don't tell me when to and what to do no more."
I listen.
I'm listening . . .

OSHOOSI SIZE

You left me?

OGUN SIZE

So you got to get up when you get up—

OSHOOSI SIZE

Interrupts.
I looked around and you was gone.

OGUN SIZE

Not when nobody else tell you.

OSHOOSI SIZE

I walked here . . .

OGUN SIZE

You can't get up lessen you want to, no way.

OSHOOSI SIZE

It was hot.

OGUN SIZE

I can't get up for you.

OSHOOSI SIZE

I'll see you at the house.

OGUN SIZE

Yeah
Realizing . . .
You walked?

ELEGBA

Elegba enters.

ELEGBA AND OSHOOSI

Hell yeah!

OSHOOSI SIZE

Hot as hell out there.

ELEGBA

Breathing hard . . .

OSHOOSI SIZE

What's up Legba?

ELEGBA

I had to push her here . . .

OGUN SIZE

Push who?

ELEGBA

I had to push her most of the way . . .
She wouldn't go up on me . . .

OGUN SIZE

What you talking about?

OSHOOSI SIZE

A Realization.
A Car.

ELEGBA

A Car.

OGUN SIZE

A Car?
Where?

ELEGBA

She down there.
A couldn't get her up that hill.

OSHOOSI SIZE

Hell I barely made it up that hill.

OGUN SIZE

But you made it.

ELEGBA

Me and no car wasn't gon make it.

OSHOOSI SIZE

Excited as hell!
A Car!

ELEGBA

Can you look at her Og?

OGUN SIZE

You got money?

OSHOOSI SIZE

Ey!

OGUN SIZE

What?

ELEGBA

I can pay you tell me what's wrong.

OGUN SIZE

Down the hill?
Will it start?

ELEGBA

Yeah.

OGUN SIZE

Ogun exits.

OSHOOSI SIZE

Sorry about that.

ELEGBA

What?

OSHOOSI SIZE

Him, man, he can be hard sometimes.

ELEGBA

It's all right.
You got a car?

OSHOOSI SIZE

Nah.

ELEGBA

Take this one.

OSHOOSI SIZE

What you mean man?

ELEGBA

OSHOOSI SIZE

What you doing?

ELEGBA

Nothing!

OSHOOSI SIZE

Why you giving me a car?

ELEGBA

Well I ain't giving it to you . . .

OSHOOSI SIZE

Where it come from?

ELEGBA

I found it.

OSHOOSI SIZE

Nigga!
C'mon, Legba you found a car?

ELEGBA

In my cousin's dump.

OSHOOSI SIZE

What I'ma do with a car that don't work?

OGUN SIZE

Excited breathing heavy.
It's fine . . .

ELEGBA

It's fine . . .

OSHOOSI SIZE

It's fine?

OGUN SIZE

Better than fine.
That car in good shape.
The outside beat up . . .
But even that's a cool blue
All you got to do is polish that up.
You ain't have no problems with cars like that . . .
Yeah you got to tune it up sometimes . . .
Pop it when it's buckin on you
But those one of those American Classics.
Those "I will run longer and stronger than the human
Body" cars. Man please that car got plenty run in it.

OSHOOSI SIZE

Why Legba couldn't get her to run?

ELEGBA

I ain't got no license.

OSHOOSI SIZE

Nigga you don't know how to drive?

ELEGBA

I mean I do.
I think I do still remember.
But my license still suspended.
Gotta get a new one.
Beside I ran into the Law the other day.

OSHOOSI SIZE

Oh shit.

> OGUN SIZE

Ah nah.

> ELEGBA

Yeah.

> OSHOOSI SIZE

What he say?

> OGUN SIZE

He say something to you?

> ELEGBA

What he always say?

> OSHOOSI SIZE, OGUN SIZE AND ELEGBA

"Eh Boy . . .

> OGUN SIZE

"What you doing round here?"

> OSHOOSI SIZE

"Stay out of the shit fore you start to stink."

> ELEGBA

"What you doing?
Where you going?
Better be quick."

> OGUN SIZE

I swear that man ain't neva gon change.

> OSHOOSI SIZE

Anytime he see another black man in
Town he act like he got to chase him out.

ELEGBA

Sheriff act like he the only nigga
Can be seen in the town.

OSHOOSI SIZE

He ask you questions too Og?

OGUN SIZE

Man you know he treat everybody like
We guilty till proven innocent.

ELEGBA

Cept them white folks.

OSHOOSI SIZE

Nothing but, "How do sir."

OGUN SIZE

"Morning."

ELEGBA

"Morning, sir.
Yall might want take shed of this sun lessen
You want to get as dark as me today.
Ha ha ha!"

OSHOOSI SIZE

And they laugh too.

ELEGBA

Yeah they do.

OGUN SIZE

Laugh with the darkie play play sheriff.

OSHOOSI SIZE

Laugh nigga laugh.

OGUN SIZE

"Lessen you want to get as dark as me."

ELEGBA

He see me see him.

OSHOOSI SIZE

Huh?

ELEGBA

He see me look his way on the way to the Food Lion.
He look over his glasses.

OGUN SIZE

That smile just coming off his face I bet.

ELEGBA

The white people he talking to walk on by,
Some of the Witt boys.
They walk on by . . .
But he stay there looking at me.

OSHOOSI SIZE

He had you in sights.

OGUN SIZE

You caught him playing monkey.

OSHOOSI SIZE

That's a crime in itself.

OGUN SIZE

Punishable by death.

ELEGBA

He say, "Where you going Legba?"

OSHOOSI SIZE

He remember your name?

OGUN SIZE

He call me Size.

OSHOOSI SIZE

Call me Size too.

OGUN SIZE

Like we twins . . .

OSHOOSI SIZE

Or the same person.

OGUN SIZE

Like it's only one of us.

OSHOOSI SIZE

Like we the same.

ELEGBA

"Where you going Legba?"
"Nowhere, sir."
Huh.

OSHOOSI SIZE

Huh.

OGUN SIZE

Huh.

ELEGBA

"When they let you out?"

OSHOOSI SIZE

"Let you"?

ELEGBA

"They didn't let me do nothing.
I served my time.
Did all of it.
Got a job work at the funeral home."

OGUN SIZE

Legba you work at the . . .

OSHOOSI SIZE

Leave it lone Ogun.

ELEGBA

"You got you a job huh boy.
You think you fully rehabitulated son?"

OGUN SIZE

What?

ELEGBA

You know "rehabitulated."

OSHOOSI SIZE

What the fuck is that?

ELEGBA

Ha, the nigga trying to say "rehabilitated."

OSHOOSI SIZE

Niggas.

OGUN SIZE

Stupid nigga.

ELEGBA

"You fully rehabitulated?"
"Yes, sir, I think I am."
"You should know shouldn't you?"
"I guess."
"There you go again son, guessing, thinking . . .
That's what got you in trouble in the first place, ain't it?
Thinking you was too fast.
Thinking you could get away . . .
If you was better, you would know better than to
Think or guess ever again."

OSHOOSI SIZE

What you say Legba?

OGUN SIZE

What you say?

ELEGBA

I say, "Maybe you right, sir."
"Maybe!"

OGUN SIZE

Oh no.

OSHOOSI SIZE

Shit Legba.

ELEGBA

"Maybe I'm right huh?
Well let's go see your parole officer see if he think
I'm right."
"What fo?"
"Well you bout to go back in ain't you?"
"Why?"
"You standing here loitering."
"No, sir."
"You ain't, no?
Well you got a clear answer to that."
"Yes, sir."
"Don't let me catch you running Legba."
"Sir?"
"Don't stand still and don't run . . .
Don't wanna see you riding or flying . . .
Every time I see you I better see you
Getting where you need to go,
Where you should be going,
The way God intended for you to get there,
Before the modern inventions of life made it
Easier for the scum of the earth to transport they evil deeds.
Back when all you had was your feet to the earth . . .
Don't let your transgressions vine up around you son . . ."

OSHOOSI SIZE

"Don't let the weeds of the world strangle you."

OGUN SIZE

"The mud . . ."

ELEGBA
"Don't let it stick you and choke you."

OSHOOSI SIZE, OGUN SIZE AND ELEGBA
"Don't play in the shit you'll start to stink."

ELEGBA
"Yes, sir."

OSHOOSI SIZE
"Yes, sir."

OGUN SIZE
Huh.

ELEGBA
That's when the Witt boys came back.
Asked him if they could have a ride half back to the house.
They say they taken his advice trying not to catch sunstroke
Walking back home.
"You good boys come on catch a ride."
Smiling.

OSHOOSI SIZE
Beaming huh.

OGUN SIZE
Big smile.

ELEGBA
That M&M kind of smile.

OSHOOSI SIZE

Oshoosi stares at Elegba
Like someone who just heard
A ghost or remembered a dream.

ELEGBA

You know, like they just asked to blow sunshine up his ass.

OGUN SIZE

Might do.

OSHOOSI SIZE

Huh.

ELEGBA

So I decided to push her over rather than risk getting
    caught riding?

OSHOOSI SIZE

Nigga you crazy.

ELEGBA

How much you want for looking at her Size Number One?

OGUN SIZE

Nothing man.
It's cool.

ELEGBA

Ey thanks Ogun, man, that's nice of you.

OSHOOSI SIZE

Yeah man.

OGUN SIZE

Yeah well enjoy your car Legba.
Get somebody teach you how to drive it.
Don't see how you can with the
Law pressin you . . .

ELEGBA

It ain't mine.

OGUN SIZE

I thought you just said . . .

ELEGBA

I brought it here for Osi.

OGUN SIZE	OSHOOSI SIZE
A Car?	A Car.

ELEGBA

Yeah. Man.
Here.
Here.

ACT 2

SCENE 1

Oshoosi Size and Elegba follow the action described by Ogun Size.

OGUN SIZE

A week later . . .
Ogun Size is sleeping,
Dreaming.

OGUN SIZE

OGUN SIZE

And in his dream
Is his brother Oshoosi
And his friend Legba.

OSHOOSI SIZE

ELEGBA

OGUN SIZE

In this dream of Ogun's
There is something strange
Happening.
His brother Oshoosi and Legba
Are bound together.
And they seem to want to part ways,
To separate.
But they can't.

OSHOOSI SIZE

ELEGBA

OGUN SIZE

They can't seem to get loose of one another,

OSHOOSI SIZE

ELEGBA

For a moment
In this dream of Ogun's
It seems that Elegba has changed
His heart.
And now stead of trying to get away from
Shoosi he staying with him,
Doing everything he can to be next to him.
And now Shoosi looking confused . . .

OSHOOSI SIZE

ELEGBA

OGUN SIZE

Not knowing what to do,
Where to go, how to move,
Just feeling trapped.

Ogun wants to tell his brother
To call him . . .
Call me Shoosi I will help you.

But it's too late.
Ogun's dream ends
And Elegba is dragging
His brother Oshoosi along with him
And there ain't nothing he can do about it!

SCENE 2

OGUN SIZE

Ogun waking up.
OSI!

OSHOOSI SIZE

Coming in.
What?

OGUN SIZE

Oshoosi?
You, you still here?

OSHOOSI SIZE

What's wrong Og?
Man you sweatin.

199

OGUN SIZE

Yeah I was just . . .
Sleeping . . .

OSHOOSI SIZE

You sleeping that's some shit.
Ey man listen thank you for the car man.

OGUN SIZE

Well see that's . . .
The thing . . . I mean I fixed it for you.

OSHOOSI SIZE

I know, I know . . . I need a job.
I think the Food Lion is gon be my best bet.

OGUN SIZE

That's . . .

OSHOOSI SIZE

Man I damn sure don't want to . . .
But ey, wouldn't be called work if I wanted
To do it.

OGUN SIZE

Lil brother . . .

OSHOOSI SIZE

But you got a career in the cars man . . .

OGUN SIZE

Yeah I love fixing . . .

OSHOOSI SIZE

I need to find something like that for myself.

OGUN SIZE

Like? You can . . .

OSHOOSI SIZE

I was thinking about going to school.

OGUN SIZE

Oh. Oh yeah?

OSHOOSI SIZE

Yeah man take some classes take one of them aptitude tests
    or something . . .
I took something like that in the pen . . .
You know it said something like I should work in social work.
I'm supposed to be sensitive to other people's needs and
    shit . . .

OGUN SIZE

Nigga . . .

OSHOOSI SIZE

Ha I'm serious.
I just want to find something like you got . . .
But with lots of vacations time man . . .
In the pen I would sit in the library . . .

OGUN SIZE

Oshoosi . . .

OSHOOSI SIZE

They had this one book was this big-ass book full of pictures
    of Madagascar.

I mean just the people, the places, the water, the eating, the
ground the earth, the fucking, fecundity!

OGUN SIZE

Fe . . .
"Fecundity"?

OSHOOSI SIZE

You like that!

OGUN SIZE

Ha, yeah!

OSHOOSI SIZE

All these black-and-white and color pictures no words.
One of the reasons why I picked it up probably . . .
I'ma start reading more!
I ain't no idiot, I mean I should read about this world . . .
I wanna go.

OGUN SIZE

Osi.

OSHOOSI SIZE

I want to go to Madagascar!
Hell I wanna go to Mexico man it's right there!
Right there and I ain't ever been.

OGUN SIZE

What?

OSHOOSI SIZE

You know what fucked me up Og?
This what got me man . . .

I am looking at this book and I am thinking wow this place
   look far away, far as hell . . .
This place out there, these people ain't even got on no
   clothes hardly and then I see it.

OGUN SIZE

What?

OSHOOSI SIZE

This man . . .
This nigga . . .
This man . . .
He look just like me!
I swear somebody trying to fuck with me . . .
Legba or the warden done got a picture of me and stuck it in
   this book about Madagascar with me half naked n shit . . .
But it ain't!
Him and me could've been twins man!
He standing and you know what he saying . . .
What it look like he saying?
"Come on let's go."
I can see it in his eyes!
I need to be out there looking for the me's.
He got something to tell me man.
Something about me that I don't know 'cause I am living
   here and all I see here are faces telling me what's wrong
   with me.
Maybe the me in China can tell me why I can't sleep at night.
Shit man who knows . . .
Man!
Ha. Ha.
I smoked too much today. Talking shit, right?

OGUN SIZE

Nah man you not talking . . .
Wait you smoked?

OSHOOSI SIZE

Yeah just a lil bit . . .

OGUN SIZE

Osi . . .

OSHOOSI SIZE

Don't worry about it.
The Food Lion don't give drug tests, besides it's weed . . .

OGUN SIZE

I know . . .

OSHOOSI SIZE

I love what you did to the ride man.
That shit is . . . it's beautiful.
I love you for it.

OGUN SIZE

It's yours but . . .

OSHOOSI SIZE

Man . . . I'm going be real careful in it.

OGUN SIZE

Please . . .

OSHOOSI SIZE

Me and Legba just going to the outlet . . .
Gon see what's playing at the pictures.

Mostly going to see the women that come out for the pictures.
Hell ain't nothing out really that I want to see.
Would like to see some thongs walk by.
And once they see me and Legba and that sparkling ride
    they wanna show me they panny line.
I am down for inspection.

ELEGBA

From outside:
Beep.

OGUN SIZE

What the hell?

OSHOOSI SIZE

That must be Legba out there fucking around.

OGUN SIZE

Ey man . . .

OSHOOSI SIZE

Laughing. To Elegba:
Ey man!
Nigga.

OGUN SIZE

Osi . . .

OSHOOSI SIZE

I got it Og.

ELEGBA

Beep.

OSHOOSI SIZE

Ha ha!
Ey nigga!
Stop wearing out my horn I'm coming.
They arrest niggas just for that these days . . .
Get your arm out my window.

OGUN SIZE

Osi.

OSHOOSI SIZE

Yeah Og?

ELEGBA

Beep.

OSHOOSI SIZE

Keep on Crazy Kat.

OGUN SIZE

Ey.

OSHOOSI SIZE

I'ma be fine . . .
Fo sho.
Go back to sleep Og.
Go head.
Oshoosi exits.

SCENE 3

ELEGBA

Elegba standing the next morning, outside
At Oshoosi's window.
Oshoosi, calling . . .
Oshoosi Size.
You hear me . . .
I know you do . . .
If you in there I know you hear what Legba say.

OGUN SIZE

Ogun Size enters.
He sees Elegba at his brother's window.

ELEGBA

Hey . . . Size Number One,
How you doin?

OGUN SIZE

Morning Legba . . .
Oshoosi still sleep, man.

ELEGBA

So he here . . .

OGUN SIZE

You need something?

ELEGBA

You saw him? He here?

OGUN SIZE

Legba.

ELEGBA

I just want to tell him something.

OGUN SIZE

What, it can't wait till . . .

ELEGBA

OGUN SIZE

ELEGBA

OGUN SIZE

What you . . .

ELEGBA

Why you up so early?

OGUN SIZE

What you come to tell my brother?

ELEGBA

Ask him.

OGUN SIZE

So you got riddles for me this day
Legba.

ELEGBA

You should be sleeping or something . . .
It's still night it's so early.

OGUN SIZE

You got something to say . . .

ELEGBA

I told you who I come for

OGUN SIZE

Well he in my house and I say he sleep.

ELEGBA

Keep him there . . . locked up in your spot
Size Number One
'Cause if the Law catch him . . .

OGUN SIZE

ELEGBA

Go in the house Ogun.
You don't know who you run into this late at night,
This early in the morning.

OGUN SIZE

I run into you Legba.
I run into you.

ELEGBA

How come you never like me Size Number One?

OGUN SIZE

Legba

ELEGBA

Eh where Oshoosi get his voice? Your mama had
A voice?

OGUN SIZE

You trying to pull some bullshit?
You trying something else?

ELEGBA

I been wondering since lockup how Oshoosi get
His voice.

OGUN SIZE

You got something going on
Man.

ELEGBA

Nigga can sang!

OGUN SIZE

I swear if I find out later and you
Could have told me when I see you
I'm put my foot through you clean!

ELEGBA

First time I heard it he was hollering for you.

OGUN SIZE

ELEGBA

Yeah didn't know that; wouldn't know that.
He had just got in there good.
He hadn't been in there that long 't all
But he was strong.
Quiet to hisself.
To hisself always, but everybody break somewhere.

And one night, one night, he . . . call for you . . .
One night he just say, "I want my brother
Somebody call my brother . . ."
This grown man this man,

Crying for his brother . . .
Sobbing into the night,
"Og come for Shoosi now . . . "
At first I thought they gon get him for that
They gon hurt him for being so soft
But nah, there was a wail in that call,
And he just singing your name. Growling it
Like from somewhere I can't see but I can feel it
'Cause it's killing me. You hear dat? Killing me.

Calling for his brother. Crying for his brother.
Can't do nothing but grieve for a man who miss his brother
    like that
Sound like a bear trapped, sanging
Can't mock no man in that much earthly pain.
He make us all miss our brothers,
The ones we ain't neva even have
All the jailhouse quiet,
The guards stop like a funeral coming down the halls
In respect, respect of this man mourning the loss of his
    brother
And you just hear the clanging of that voice, like a trumpet
    shot
Out o God's Heaven
Bouncing on the cement and the steel . . . chiming like a bell
Tell he calm down . . . tell he just whispering your name
    now . . .
My brother . . . my brother . . . where my brother . . .
Gurgling it up out from under the tears . . .
My brother . . .
I can't never be his brother like you his brother.
Never.
You know that right.

No need to hate Legba.
I can't stop you from being his brother.

OGUN SIZE

ELEGBA
The Law might come round this morning.
He might come round here looking for a Size.
I ain't saying which one.
Not sure if he know which Size he want.
But seeing as how he ain't got you . . .
Must be another Size he want try on.
Must be another Size he ain't catch up with yet.
Always a way to go.
Gon head to work Ogun.
Gon to your shop.

OGUN SIZE

ELEGBA
Go on.

OGUN SIZE
Ogun exits.

SCENE 4

OGUN SIZE
Slam.
Since day one . . .
Day one . . .

You been fucking-up . . .
Not just the other day when you was standing here,
Looking all lost and stupid; all high on life
And the little bit of weed that Food Lion won't find in your
    piss.
Nah hell nah.
FROM DAY ONE.
Aunt Elegua stopped taking us to church.
I stopped going 'cause I ain't want to go in the first place.
But you kept getting up in the morning, you kept getting
    up every Sabbath,
And going down to the river to wash your fucking sins
    away . . .
And everybody say, "Look at Little Size taking up the cross
    with Jesus."
"Look at him he only nine."
"Look at that devotion for Jesus!"
"You should do like your brother Ogun . . . You should go to
    church like Shoosi!"
You know what I wanted to say? "Fuck that nigga and the
    church."
I was jealous.
I wanted to be you for a moment, Little Size, I wanted to be
    just like my Little Brother until me and Elegua found
    you using the money you was stealing from collection in
    a crap game.
Yeah. Yeah.
And then everything turned.
Everything turned. Spun right round. Landed on me.
Everybody like, "He only nine."
"If you would have been a better role model for him Ogun
    he wouldn't acted like this."
"If I would've . . . If I . . ."

Aunt Elegua sealed it though . . . that miserable old-ass
   lady . . .
She say, "Your mama would have been so disappointed in
   you . . . Letting your brother go like that. Yemoja would
   have hated you failing her Ogun. Letting Your Brother
   Go." Letting you go . . . I let you go? I let you go. I got
   one image of my mama in my mind, one . . . and it fucks
   with me at night . . .
She standing near the water, my mama standing out look-
   ing out, looking out towards the gulf, belly full of you
   and she standing there holding my hand.
Tight.
Tight.
Tight.
Just her and the water . . .
Us. That's all I got left of my mama, and you in that pic-
   ture.
You a part of all I got left nigga.
So I held on from that day . . .
I gripped onto your ass and pushed you through school . . .
   I forced you up and out . . .
Whatever the fuck you . . . I did it . . . I burned my chance
at anything so that I didn't leave you behind . . . I would
run after you and ahead of you always hoping that I could
keep my grip on you or at least catch you before anyone
else did.
But no matter what I did . . . No matter if I thought you
were fine . . . I thought you were gonna be okay somehow
you would slip through and fuck up and fuck up and fuck
up and when you fucked up somehow I fucked up! Some
how there is no escaping you! You say I ain't never been in
the pen? Nigga whenever you fall everyone look at me like
I fucking pushed you . . . That's my fucking life sentence . . .

That's my lockdown . . . All my life I carry your sins on my
back . . . And now you out there riding around in a car that
I suped up and popped off only so they could find you in it
with a fucking pound of powder! Cocaine!
What the fuck?

OSHOOSI SIZE

It wasn't mine Ogun . . .

OGUN SIZE

Shut up! Shut up, shut the fuck up. You shut up don't say a
fucking . . . You fucked up . . . Say that! You wanna say
something for once in your life say something for me . . .
You fucked up, you fucked up, you fucked up, you fucked
up you fucked up you fucked up you fucked up you fucked
up you fucked up you fucked up you fucked up you fucked
up you fucked up you fucked up you fucked up.

You fucked up!

OSHOOSI SIZE

I.

OGUN SIZE

You fucked up

OSHOOSI SIZE

He . . .

OGUN SIZE

You fucked up

OSHOOSI SIZE

I fucked up.

OGUN SIZE

OSHOOSI SIZE

OGUN SIZE

So what you doin in here, hiding out?

OSHOOSI SIZE

I ain't did nothing.

OGUN SIZE

What he lying?
Say he lying.
I swear . . . please tell me how?
If you convince me he lying I'm with you . . .
Tell me how he lying Oshoosi!
The Law running around here . . .
Looking for you . . .
I . . . don't wanna know . . .
Yeah I do . . .
But . . . I . . .
You gotta . . .
You have to . . .
Please . . .
You have to . . . C'mon . . .

OSHOOSI SIZE

Legba and me was going to the outlet. He had a gym bag
    out there said he had to spend the night near the Bayou.
Said his Cousin Nia was gon let him stay with her for a
    while out by the water.
The night was going good Ogun you know . . .
It was right . . .

We left the pictures, we look at the girls for a minute, few of
em smiling . . . few of em laughing. But you know he want
me to drive out there, wanted me to go out there . . . And
drop him off.
So I say okay.
What laws I break?
I drove too fast out to Nia's. Yeah that I did do. 'Cause
I remembered how phyne . . . I wanted to see if I could get
at her. I had sin on my mind but not in my heart. So I was
racing . . . And I'm just going and I got the wind coming in
the car and the songs playing and Legba laughing, 'cause
we having a good time . . . It's nice out . . . ain't too hot
yet . . . And . . . and I'm driving and singing.
(Sings)
Just feel right that they played it.
(Sings)
I can feel Nia singing it to me you know. Inviting me to
spend the night too. I'm singing and I caught a breeze
right in my nose, that brackish water breeze right in my
fucking nose and I sneezed . . . and the car spun right
round. And I stopped and snot was hanging out my nose,
I was laughing my ass off, it was so funny. Legba was
laughing and it was dark and shit . . . It was real dark and
laughing and then . . . And then felt like a fucking dream.
Music still playing.

ELEGBA

Elegba enters, singing.
(Sings)
Ogun stands watching.

OSHOOSI SIZE

I felt like I had been there before.

217

(Elegba sings.)

OSHOOSI SIZE

Just us out there . . . Just the car sitting and chillin hearing
that ol music . . . hearing it say something but really just
telling me that I'm free and everything all right . . . Legba
say, Legba say,

ELEGBA

This nice man.

OSHOOSI SIZE

I say yeah man.
Yeah it is.
He say let's . . .

ELEGBA

Let's just sit for a minute . . .

OSHOOSI SIZE

I say all right man
But no too long gotta get to your cousin.

ELEGBA

Yeah but this nice, right?

OSHOOSI SIZE

He say this nice . . .
I say yeah man you right. It was Ogun. I ain't gon lie. I never
felt like that. I smell that Gulf air. Just making me think
more of Nia. Remember her body. Music making me sleepy.

(Elegba sings.)

OSHOOSI SIZE

Making me sleepy and hard at the same time . . . Why that
happen Ogun, why when you get sleepy yo dick hard?
Guess that mystery to be solved by scientist and astrologers
or people who got plenty of time to study dick . . . All this a
dream it was so quiet out there . . .

(Elegba sings.
Elegba and Oshoosi Size sing.
Oshoosi Size sings.)

ELEGBA

Elegba touches Oshoosi head.

OSHOOSI SIZE

It couldn't been happening.

ELEGBA

Let's, let's stay for a second.
Legba's hand rests on Shoosi shoulder.

OSHOOSI SIZE

Not for real . . .

(Elegba sings.)

ELEGBA

His hand slides down . . .

OSHOOSI SIZE

Not like that.

(Elegba sings.)

ELEGBA

Slides down onto his thigh.

OSHOOSI SIZE

What you doin?

ELEGBA

Elegba smiling.
Nothing brother . . .
Just singing to you like I used to.
This nice ain't it?

OSHOOSI SIZE

ELEGBA

Right?

(Elegba sings.)

OSHOOSI SIZE

And then I heard sirens.
Come out nowhere lights and sirens.
Music playing.
The Law come up on us looking like he happy bout some-
    thing.
With that gotcha face on.
Shining his light.
"You got anything in the trunk son?"
"No, sir."
Nothing was in there as far as I know.
"No, sir."
"Well what in the shit is this?"
I hate how some niggas don't know how to cuss right.

Who say, "What in the shit"?
"What in the shit is this?"
He standing hold this bag wide open.
He ain't supposed to search the car unless he got provocation.
But damnit if the sheriff ain't standing there holding
    Legba's bag
It's pouring white out onto the asphalt.
I wish you could've seen my face . . .
I like to jump over and kill Legba
But the Law say get out that car.
I say, "Legba what the fuck he holding man?
What you doing?"
He just looking.
Almost like he smiling.
And I see where he at already . . . I see where Legba at.
He in jail. He already sitting in his cell singing.

(Elegba sings.)

OSHOOSI SIZE

He back there just that fast.

(Elegba sings.)

OSHOOSI SIZE

And I see him go there . . .
I see them walls around him . . .

(Elegba sings.)

OSHOOSI SIZE

I see them dark-ass halls and the midnights with no sleep.
I swear I see em Ogun as you my brother I see em.

(Elegba sings.)

OSHOOSI SIZE

And I can't.

I just can't.

So I ran.

I can't tell you what I ran like, how I ran . . . what I saw
    when I ran . . .

I ran . . .

I run all the way till I get here.

And I come in here and I close the door and I say I ain't
going back . . .

I ain't going back.

OGUN SIZE

Ogun Size stares at his brother.

OSHOOSI SIZE

Oshoosi Size his younger brother.

OSHOOSI SIZE

I am here now . . . Brother Size . . .

I'm here. What we gon do?

SCENE 5

OGUN SIZE

That same night.

OSHOOSI SIZE

Later on.

OGUN SIZE

Nigga you lying!

OSHOOSI SIZE

You trying to tell me you ain't say it?

OGUN SIZE

I ain't neva said no shit like . . .

OSHOOSI SIZE

I remember it like it was yesterday.
Roon had just came round the house and told us that
    Mama finally passed.
I was little but I wasn't that damn little.
He say, "She gone Ele. Yemoja finally let go."
Roon turn around and see us standing there and walk over
    to us.
And he said, "Lil men yo mama ain't coming here to get you.
She went to be a part of the number.
She went on with the father now.
Yall don't be sad or scared.
Yo mama ain't coming."
He say, "You understand, lil man?"
Getting all close in my face breath smelling like snuff . . .
All Loud:
"YOU UNDERSTAND, LIL MAN?"
I say, "Yeah I hear you.
Anything to get yo ass out my face.
I gotcha."
He look at you he say, "You be strong Ogun."
And I swear you could see the tremor start in your face . . .

OGUN SIZE

Ha-hah!
Shut up . . .

OSHOOSI SIZE

Like the Mississippi swelling up.
You so ugly when you cry.
If you cried today I still bet it's ugly . . .
You say . . .

OGUN SIZE

Go on now.

OSHOOSI SIZE

You say,
"LORD GOD . . . WILL THIS PAIN . . . EVER GO AWAY?!"
Knees buckled from under you.
Falling on the ground grabbing up the carpet underneath you.
Convulsing and weeping and wailing like Mary.
I like to cried 'cause I thought you was finna die.
I say, "Lord you done took my mama not my brother too."

OGUN SIZE

Ha-hah!
It ain't funny Oshoosi
I was in grief.

OSHOOSI SIZE

Your ass was overdramatic!

OGUN SIZE

Hah!

OSHOOSI SIZE

Then Aunt Ele kept calling you carpet boy for so long after.

OGUN SIZE

That woman don't got a sympathetic bone in her
Body.

OSHOOSI SIZE

But damn sure got a lotta body.

OGUN SIZE

You ain't neva lied.

OSHOOSI SIZE

Then gon have the nerve to have a fainting spell at mama's
funeral.
Fat ass . . .

OGUN SIZE

Like somebody could hold her big ass up.

OSHOOSI SIZE

Thank God for O Li Roon
Because I wasn't about to try and revive her nothing.
Her big ass passed out,
I say, "Let her stay out that teach her ass for fainting."
I wasn't going nowhere near her.

OGUN SIZE

Hateful Aunt Elegua.

OSHOOSI SIZE

Sitting over there old as she wanna be.
Like she ain't never gon die.
Walking Negro spirtual.
Just keep rolling along.

OGUN SIZE

Seem like she never liked us,
Liked she resented Mama for getting sick
And having to take us in.

OSHOOSI SIZE

Wasn't like we didn't come with two nice welfare checks
To go long with us.
Hell the government might as well put money clips round
    us and handed us to her.

OGUN SIZE

And she still gypped us at Christmas.

OSHOOSI SIZE

Ain't that some shit?
Thank God for Santa Claus.

OGUN SIZE

You believe in Santa?

OSHOOSI SIZE

My big brother leaving me presents under the tree . . .
Yeah I believe.

OGUN SIZE

You knew it was me?

OSHOOSI SIZE

Who else it gon be?
Nobody else care.
You act like you don't care . . .
You act like you so tough but I would catch it . . .

I catch you looking at me sometimes like you wanna beat
  my ass you so mad.
Then I see this smile crack.
I see it and I see you . . .

OGUN SIZE

OSHOOSI SIZE

OGUN SIZE

What you do in prison?

OSHOOSI SIZE

Man why you always ask that?

OGUN SIZE

You know what I do when you was gone . . .

OSHOOSI SIZE

OGUN SIZE

Think about what you was doing right then.
Sometimes I see you in there smiling big.
That's one thing about you I do know . . .
You kind to everybody.
You give everybody a chance and yeah you fuck up but
  that's how the world balance you out.
All that niceness you pass to everybody they take it and it
  comes back so that when you do fuck up you paying for
  it ain't so bad.
You good to everybody you meet.
Only thing prison made you was tired.

OSHOOSI SIZE

You right Og, I'm tired man. So tired.
Tired. Too tired to fight it off.

OGUN SIZE

Ogun staring at his brother not knowing what to say.

OSHOOSI SIZE

Oshoosi looking at the ground thinking of all he done said . . .

OGUN SIZE

Nothing more to say . . .

OSHOOSI SIZE

Weary of saying anything.

OGUN SIZE

Weary of talking.

OSHOOSI SIZE AND OGUN SIZE

Weary.

(Ogun Size sings.)

OSHOOSI SIZE

Aw hell nah.
I'm already on the cusp of crazy you trying to push me over.

OGUN SIZE

What?

OSHOOSI SIZE

Nigga you know you can't sing.

OGUN SIZE

Ey, the song just popped into my head.

OSHOOSI SIZE

Pop it out.

OGUN SIZE

Ey, I use to sing you to sleep.

OSHOOSI SIZE

No I use to close my ears until I passed out.

OGUN SIZE

Ha.
You the singer.

OSHOOSI SIZE

Nah man you crazy.

OGUN SIZE

Sing that song for me I want to hear it.

OSHOOSI SIZE

Nah c'mon Og.

OGUN SIZE

You ain't sleeping no time soon.
Me neither.
C'mon sing for me.

OSHOOSI SIZE

OGUN SIZE

OSHOOSI SIZE

I tell you what . . .

OGUN SIZE

What?

OSHOOSI SIZE

Play backup for me.

OGUN SIZE

What!

OSHOOSI SIZE

Don't act like you ain't never done it before.

OGUN SIZE

Where you going?

OSHOOSI SIZE

Hold the hell on.
Coming.
I'll be right there.
Turns on music.

OGUN SIZE

That sweet song start playing.
I didn't know you had this song.

OSHOOSI SIZE

Every man need a copy of this song.

OGUN SIZE

Man you use to sing the hell out of this song.

OSHOOSI SIZE

Still do.
But I need a piano man.

OGUN SIZE

You mean a organ man.

OSHOOSI SIZE

Ah nigga just play whatever but in the back.

OGUN SIZE

All right Ike I'm getting.

(Oshoosi Size sings with the music...)

OGUN SIZE

I think I'ma switch to drums.

OSHOOSI SIZE

Good work brother.

OGUN SIZE

I thought you would enjoy that brother.
C'mon sing the song.

(Oshoosi Size sings.)

OGUN SIZE

Yeah!

(Oshoosi Size sings.)

OGUN SIZE

What you got do?

251

(Oshoosi Size sings. Then Ogun Size and Oshoosi Size sing together.)

OSHOOSI SIZE

Laughing.
Eh you kinda overstepping your boundaries piano/sax man.

OGUN SIZE

Having a good time . . .
Eh man I am just backing you up.
Just sing the song Anna Mae.

(Oshoosi Size sings.)

OGUN SIZE

Now you getting into it!
But don't turn into a Temptation.
Keep it cool.

OSHOOSI SIZE

Let me do this!

OGUN SIZE

You got it.

(Oshoosi Size sings.)

OGUN SIZE

Playing backup and
Doing Temptation moves.

*(Oshoosi Size sings. Laughs!
Ogun Size cracks up!*

Oshoosi Size sings.
Ogun Size smiles.
Oshoosi Size sings.)

ELEGBA

Elegba appears at the window,
Like a glimmer of moonlight,
For a moment is gone.

OSHOOSI SIZE

Oshoosi sees it.
How could he not?
He stops singing.

OGUN SIZE

What happened?

OSHOOSI SIZE

Tired.
Voice tired.

OGUN SIZE

C'mon man finish.

OSHOOSI SIZE

I can't man.

OGUN SIZE

Eh brother just try to . . .

OSHOOSI SIZE

Eh man I'm done . . .

                              OGUN SIZE

But Oshoo you . . .
C'mon man you the star.
Shine little brother . . .

                              OSHOOSI SIZE

I don't want to play no more.

                              OGUN SIZE

Brother . . .

                              OSHOOSI SIZE

Eh, stop pushing me Og.
I said I am done man.
I'm going to bed.

                              OGUN SIZE

                              OSHOOSI SIZE

Oshoosi Size exits to bed.

                              OGUN SIZE

Ogun Size is left alone.
Without his brother.
The music plays in the background.

The music turns off.
Just the sound of night, now.

Okay man.
Okay.
Good night.

Ogun Size stands alone in the night.
Staring.

OGUN SIZE

OGUN SIZE

OGUN SIZE

OGUN SIZE

OGUN SIZE

OGUN SIZE

OGUN SIZE

And the next morning . . .

SCENE 6

OGUN SIZE

Ogun Size enters.
Osi!
Calling for his brother.
Osi . . .
Oshoosi Size!

OSHOOSI SIZE

Waking up.
Og man
Why you calling!

OGUN SIZE

Get up.

OSHOOSI SIZE

What time is it!

OGUN SIZE

Time to go.

OSHOOSI SIZE

What you talking about man!

OSHOOSI SIZE

What you doin . . .

OGUN SIZE

THROW!

OSHOOSI SIZE

Eh man that's all my shit!

OGUN SIZE

Get it together . . .

OSHOOSI SIZE

Brother . . . Brother Size man . . .

OGUN SIZE

You got to get outta here.

OSHOOSI SIZE

You just . . .
You upset!
What you mad at?
What, you don't believe me?
Og!

Ogun!
Man . . . don't do me like this!

OGUN SIZE

Get your shit.
Get in the truck.

OSHOOSI SIZE

Og.

OGUN SIZE

Don't come back.
Don't call here.
Don't write . . .
When they come here . . .
When the Law comes here for you . . .
I'm going to deny you . . .
They gon ask for my brother . . .
I'm going to say I ain't got none . . .
He gon say there two Size,
I'm gon say nah, just one. Only one . . .
I'ma deny you . . .
Up to three times . . .
That's all I can take.
That's how many times I can do it . . .
Don't cry when you hear about it . . .
Don't think I don't know you . . .
Don't believe it . . . Hear me . . .
You here with me . . .
Always . . .
But you gotta go fore you get caught . . . .
Get in the truck, all your shit brother . . .
Everything you need . . .

Need Shoosi need . . .
Only stop when you need . . .
So don't stop till you free . . .
Don't stop . . .
Open your hand.

OSHOOSI SIZE

What!

OGUN SIZE

Open your hand!

OSHOOSI SIZE

Okay . . .

OGUN SIZE

This it . . .
This everything . . .
All I got it's yours.
Here Oshoosi.

OSHOOSI SIZE

Og man don't do this . . .

OGUN SIZE

It's done . . .
Get in the truck . . .
Take it . . .
Go south . . .
See Mexico.

OSHOOSI SIZE

Mexico . . .

OGUN SIZE

It's right there and you ain't never been . . . right?

OSHOOSI SIZE

OGUN SIZE

What you waiting on man?

OSHOOSI SIZE

OGUN SIZE

Man don't let them put you back in there.
I wanna know you still my brother somewhere . . .
Anywhere in the world.
You still my brother . . .
I swear.
Out there you will still be a Size, Oshoosi Size
Brother to Ogun.

OSHOOSI SIZE

OGUN SIZE

I fixed the truck for you.
If it act up on you,
If it start bucking don't stop,
Hit it and call my name.
The truck know me . . .
It'll carry you on . . .

OSHOOSI SIZE

Oshoosi Size breaking down . . .

OGUN SIZE

Ogun trying to hold it.
It's all right . . .
It's all right brother.
It's gon be all right.
I believe you.
I do.
Just go.
Go find you.
When you meet him,
Ask him if he remember me.
Ask him.
Ask.

OSHOOSI SIZE

OGUN SIZE

OSHOOSI SIZE

OGUN SIZE

OSHOOSI SIZE

Oshoosi Size leaves his brother Ogun Size
Standing in the early morning . . .

OGUN SIZE

Ogun Size sees it, how can he not, and is left alone in the
Early fore day in the morning mist. End of play.

(Blackout.)

MARCUS;

Or the Secret of Sweet

To my best

PRODUCTION HISTORY

Marcus; Or the Secret of Sweet has been produced as part of *The Brother/Sister Plays* in numerous productions starting in 2009 (see *In the Red and Brown Water*). *Marcus; Or the Secret of Sweet* was first produced at the Yale School of Drama in 2006 as part of its first Carlotta Festival of New Plays.

CHARACTERS

MARCUS ESHU	son of Elegba and Oba, sixteen; a young man of color
OSHOOSI SIZE	a spirit, brother to Ogun Size
OBA	mother to Marcus; a young mother of color
OGUN SIZE	brother to Oshoosi Size; a man of color
OSHA	daughter of Shun and Shango, best friend of Marcus Eshu, seventeen; a young woman of color
SHAUNTA IYUN	daughter of Nia, best friend of Marcus and Osha, eighteen; a young woman of color
SHUN	mother of Osha, godmother of Shaunta Iyun; a young mother of color
ELEGUA	aunt to Ogun and Oshoosi Size; a woman of color
SHUA OR JOSHUA	from the Bronx nee Stratford, Connecticut; a man of color
TERRELL	a young man of color

PROLOGUE

A Dream

The lights come up on Marcus in his bed sleeping and Oshoosi Size standing in a pool of water crying gently at first until he covers his mouth, doubles over, and . . .

OBA

(Offstage)
Marcus . . .

(Lights out on Oshoosi. Marcus wakes breathing heavy.)

OBA

(Offstage)
Marcus!

MARCUS

Ma'am?

OBA

(Offstage)
C'mon, we gon be late!

(Shift.)

A Processional

The cast forms a funeral processional led by Ogun Size and trailed by Marcus.

OGUN SIZE

A funeral processional for Shango.
(Singing)

> Walk with me Lord!
> Walk with me.
> Walk with me Lord!
> Walk with me.
> While I am on this . . .
> Tedious journey.
> I want you Lord. To walk
> With me.

Ogun breaks down: he puts his hand to his mouth, doubles over, and cries to himself. He walks offstage. Marcus stops, stares at Ogun.

ACT 1

SCENE 1

OSHA

Marcus?

MARCUS

Ever seen a black boy stop n stare?
Like he just heard a ghost.
Or remembered a . . .

SHAUNTA IYUN AND OSHA

Marcus!

MARCUS

I . . . can't go down there.

OSHA

Why?

MARCUS

I got this feeling.

SHAUNTA IYUN

Shaunta moves to leave his butt right there.

OSHA

Shaunta?

SHAUNTA IYUN

What?

OSHA

Describe the feeling?

MARCUS

Strange like, like I been here before.

OSHA

It's a funeral . . .

SHAUNTA IYUN

We all been here before.

OSHA

Let's just go down so we get it over with.

SHAUNTA IYUN

Osha don't pull him girl let Marcus
Foolish self sit right here if he want.
This ain't your day. This ain't his day.
This your daddy, Shango, funeral, girl c'mon.

OSHA

No, wait, I barely know'd the n . . .

SHAUNTA IYUN

Osha!

OSHA

Marc . . .

SHAUNTA IYUN

Here she go.

OSHA

Osha steps to her best friend.

SHAUNTA IYUN

Ackin like he her boyfriend.

OSHA

Come down.

SHAUNTA IYUN

Boy holding us up . . .

OSHA

I need you to.

SHAUNTA IYUN

Ain't even his people's funeral.

OSHA

For me.

(Osha moves closer.)

MARCUS

Marcus uncomfortable . . .
All right!

OSHA

All right?

SHAUNTA IYUN

All right. Shoot let's . . .

(Cast, offstage, sings.)

> Oh when the saints
> Oh when the saints
> Go marching in . . .
> Hmmm.

SHAUNTA IYUN

Ain't this about a . . .
Now we done missed the damn burial.
What's wrong with you?

MARCUS

Shaunta . . .

SHAUNTA IYUN

I want to know.

MARCUS

I told you I'm tired.

OSHA

You ain't say that.

MARCUS

I . . .

OSHA AND SHAUNTA IYUN

"I . . ."

SHAUNTA IYUN

You got a secret!

MARCUS

No, I . . .
I'm just dreaming.

OSHA

Like sweet dreams?

SHAUNTA IYUN

Or beautiful nightmares?

MARCUS

Just a dream . . .

SHAUNTA IYUN

What's in it?

OSHA

Who in it?

SHUN

(Offstage)
Osha!

SHAUNTA

Ms. Shun!

OSHA

Mother of Osha . . .

MARCUS

She can't stand Marcus.

SHUN

Shun enters.
Staring at her daughter like, "She must've lost her . . ."
Through clenched teeth, "motherfuckinmind!"
Girl! How many times, too many, have I
Told you to stay away from hanging as you
Calls it with that boy, sweet Marcus, huh!

MARCUS

See.

SHUN

That's all I ask.
That's all I say. See him in school, at home
Hang with your other *girl* friends. I says it time
And time a . . . But I look up and here you go
Again down the way from the ceremony putting
Your fallen father in the fucking floor and you
Sitting here sipping on time and sunshine with
Candy Marcus! Lord! If it ain't one thing it's
Another. Osha, girl, if you don't get your ass over here!
Ooh!

OSHA

Kisses her teeth:
Stch.
I gotta go yall, she trippin.

254

SHUN

Oh I'm trippin uh, I'm falling? You wait
Till we get to this house Osha see how fast
I can get down.
Exit Shun holding hard to her stubborn child.
I done told you he just
Like his dead damn daddy, Legba.

SCENE 2

MARCUS

(To us)
Marcus stares.

SHAUNTA IYUN

Eh.

MARCUS

Huh?

SHAUNTA IYUN

Forgive her she buried her man today.

MARCUS

I'm used to it.

SHAUNTA IYUN

Too used to it.

MARCUS

She been saying it since . . .

SHAUNTA IYUN

Is it true?

MARCUS

That I'm like Legba . . .

SHAUNTA IYUN

Was he sweet?

MARCUS

Wait a . . .

SHAUNTA IYUN

Are you sweet, Marcus Eshu?

MARCUS

Marcus stung, steps back.

SHAUNTA IYUN

Marcus?

MARCUS

I heard you, Shaunta.

SHAUNTA IYUN

Seem like you ain't never gon confess it.
Surely not to Osha. You know she like you,
Huh? You know she think, "We best friends
Better lovers!" I ain't Osha. I am just your
Friend. You can tell me.

MARCUS

Wonder where that come from, calling somebody sweet?

SHAUNTA IYUN

They passed it down to us!

MARCUS

What?

SHAUNTA IYUN

BlackMoPhobia.

MARCUS

Girl you crazy . . .

SHAUNTA IYUN

Passed down from slavery.
Say the slave owners get pissed if they find
Out they slaves got gay love.
That means less children, less slaves . . . less.

MARCUS

Shaunta . . .

SHAUNTA IYUN

Think about it Marcus . . . Where else it come from?
We just naturally mad at gay folk? Come on!
Imagine it: how they got "down" back then?
Round here niggas think they got it hard on the "down low."

MARCUS

Don't say that word . . .

SHAUNTA IYUN

What about back then?
Two slaves one dark, and one light, one house
And the other field. They see each other one day.

That sparkle in they eye, they begin to gather
Together when they can, hide their love from the light.
Dark kisses in the midnight hour, with shackles for love
Bracelets, chains for promise rings. One night
Master come up on them in their secret spot 'cause
Some handkerchief-head other slave, jealous or holy, went
Off and told, "I seen't so and so House and so and so Field
Slave down together in the quarter."

                    MARCUS

You think slaves was snitchin?

                    SHAUNTA IYUN

Nosiness is primordial, snitching inevitable.

                    MARCUS

Huh.

                    SHAUNTA IYUN

Master tie and tether the lovers in front of e'rybody,
Talking bout "sending a message." Placing weights
On the their private portions. Lashing into the skin that
    they just held
To tight moments ago. Skin that was just kissed now
Split ope' from th' slash of dis white man hands.
When the wounds right he run down get some sugar
Prolly pour it on so it sting not as bad as salt but it get sticky
Melt in the singing Southern sun. Sweetness draw all the
Bugs and infection to the sores . . . Sweetness harder to
    wash. It
Become molasses in all that heat and blood and . . .

                    MARCUS

Marcus draws air . . .

SHAUNTA IYUN

That's what you dreaming about Marcus?
That's what got you waking up sweating?
You wake up scared that somebody gon catch on or . . .

MARCUS

I wake up missing my daddy.

SHAUNTA IYUN

You see him
In your dream?

MARCUS

No, that's how I know I miss him.

SHAUNTA IYUN

Shaunta leaves it for now.
All right Marc, all right.

SCENE 3

OBA

Marcus! Marcus . . .
Enter Oba calling for her son . . .

MARCUS

Whom she babies . . .

OBA

Marcus!

MARCUS

Yes, Mama?

OBA

Baby . . .

MARCUS

OBA

Where you been? I was up and down
Looking for you.

MARCUS

Sorry, I didn't feel like going to the grave.

OBA

Why, what's wrong baby?

MARCUS

I got this . . .
Mama, stop calling me baby.

OBA

But you my baby

MARCUS

Mama . . .

OBA

Marcus, you feeling all right? You got up
Two three times in the night last night.
You having movements?

MARCUS

Tell me about my daddy.

OBA

Oba's face.

Huh.

The father is in Heaven and all is right

MARCUS

No, Mama, I know all that. The Bible talks to
Me about all that but I'm talking bout my real
Daddy. Tell me bout Legba.

OBA

Why?

MARCUS

'Cause I'm asking. 'Cause you never do.

OBA

Ooh, it's hot out here, let's go.

MARCUS

It's always hot. You notice that every summer.
Some same reason it gets hot.
Shrugs.

OBA

Have you . . . Who you talking to?

MARCUS

Ma'am I'm just saying every time we get near
Bout this conversation it gets hot or the meter
Running or the chickens burning. All the time,
Every time, something starts to happen too long
When I mention the name Elegba.

                                    OBA

Huh . . .

                                    MARCUS

I just want to know about him.

                                    OBA

What you need to know?

                                    MARCUS

Am I . . . like him?

                                    OBA

Some traits we gets from our peoples are
Sleeping . . .

                                    MARCUS

The way I act.

                                    OBA

Sometimes it's better to let sleeping traits lie.

                                    MARCUS

Was he . . .

                                    OBA

What, Marcus, what?

                                    MARCUS

                                    OBA

Oba looks to the ground.
Lord.

MARCUS

Mama I . . .

OBA

I tell you this Marcus. I don't know what all the
Sudden got you on this search to find out your father
But if it's got relation to the reason why you locked
In the bathroom but not using it . . .
Or that long stare I see you, I see you, giving over
Eric down the way, you best pray on it. Think to it.
Some things are better buried. Some things left better
Unsaid. Ain't nothing sweet about a soft son.
She takes a breath.
Pick your face up off the floor, baby, and let's go.

MARCUS

I'm gonna . . . I'm gonna walk.

OBA

Huh.
She leans in.
You find your way home tonight.
When you come in you make sure you check that lil
Funky attitude at the door. You got school tomorrow.
Senior year or not. Funeral or none.
Oba exits.

A Day Dream

MARCUS

Ever had so much on your mind you forget what
You wanted to think about?
That's when it's dangerous.

Your mind starts playing on those
Things you want least to wander
Like school.
Like Latin.
Starting the second year in that class
And it's impossible to focus.

TERRELL

Enter.

TERRELL AND BOY

The boyz.

MARCUS

In this class of language there are boys from
All the teams. Focus.

TERRELL

They sit behind Marcus.

MARCUS

From basketball to track, varsity to junior.

TERRELL

Whispering:
"Marcus!"

MARCUS

And every Monday while the pop-quizzes line
The desks.

TERRELL

"Eh Marcus!"

MARCUS

The boys all lean in a lil closer.

BOY

"Sup!"

MARCUS

Trying to pick up the answers that Marcus slinging
Down.

TERRELL

"Marcus Eshu . . ."

MARCUS

They make propositions.

TERRELL

"Eh . . ."

MARCUS

Whisper in hushed, teacher-can't-hear tones:

BOY

"Let me see!"

MARCUS

Their heads yank and mouths smile.

TERRELL

"Marc . . ."

MARCUS

Motioning for me to move my head . . .

                    TERRELL
"Move your hand . . ."

                TERRELL AND BOY
"Move!"

                    MARCUS
Whispering:

                    TERRELL
"Marcus . . . Marcus!"

                    MARCUS
Focus.

                    TERRELL
But see all they want are the answers to
The test . . .

                    MARCUS
Focus . . .

                    TERRELL
Answers that will make it easier to get back to track and
    field . . .

                    MARCUS
Focus . . .

                    TERRELL
But Marcus' mind is wishin their heads were yanking and
Their mouths were asking . . .

                    MARCUS
Focus Marcus . . .

TERRELL

To, "Let me come over . . ."

MARCUS

Focus.

BOY

"Let me step closer . . ."

MARCUS

Focus.

MARCUS , TERRELL AND BOY

"Let me!"

TERRELL

Terrell and the boys fade
Like an early evening mirage.

SCENE 4

ELEGUA

Enter Elegua walking as fast as she can for near seventy.
She runs into . . .

(*Marcus stares off.*)

ELEGUA

Move boy.

MARCUS

Ms. Elegua.
Marcus moves his hand to hide his . . .

ELEGUA

Huh. She moves. Sick . . . Sick . . .

MARCUS

Ma'am!

ELEGUA

To death of funerals. Sick of em. I'm down there
Trying to pay respect to the fallen soldier and these
People having an argument ova who was his better friend.
I say, "Don't seem like none of you too good 'cause while
He was off in the war yall was over here trying to get his girl."
But I ain't say much, see, that's when I turns to Ogun,
   I say . . .

MARCUS

Ogun's down there still . . .

ELEGUA

Yeah chile. I say,
She hits the air.
"Ey let's go." "Okay." He standing there
Crying his one last cry. Lord.

MARCUS

He coming back?

ELEGUA

Who cares! I know, I ain't going to no more funerals with his
Crying ass. Making all that . . .

MARCUS

He takin it hard?

ELEGUA

Eh what the . . . I know Oba raised you better than to
Keep cutting off elders.

MARCUS

Marcus apologetic.

ELEGUA

Yeah, he taking it hard.
That's what he do, take everything to heart since
Oshoosi left.

MARCUS

Who?

ELEGUA

Ogun's brother.

MARCUS

ELEGUA

Your daddy's best . . .

MARCUS

Marcus shakes his head.

ELEGUA

Now wait a minute
This ain't no Keith sweat song, where you
Say no n I say yes. Your daddy's best was Oshoosi, Ogun's
Brother. How you don't know that?

MARCUS

It's a lot I don't know.

ELEGUA

Huh, I bet it ain't, wait.

MARCUS

What I'm waiting on?

ELEGUA

Hmmm huh. Well I wish I had the time patience
Or want withal to fill you in fella but I gots to go
This here heat make your titties sag further South
Than Violet.

MARCUS

Wait! Please . . .

ELEGUA

It's all right boi. Sometimes your mouth the last
Place words wanna go . . .

MARCUS

Was he sweet?

ELEGUA

Good evening to you too.

MARCUS

Heavy breath.
Was my daddy sweet?

ELEGUA

Ask your mama.

MARCUS

When I do she . . .

ELEGUA

Throw it off talk about something else.

MARCUS

Yeah.

ELEGUA

Your daddy liked girls enough to have you.
That ain't enough for you?

MARCUS

Yeah but . . .

ELEGUA

Listen if'n you looking for them black or white
Wrong or right answers from me honey you got
The wrong one. I just point out to you the obvious
And hope like hell you stop questioning me bout
Things I don't even much know how to explain.

MARCUS

You know how to explain dreams?

ELEGUA

Huh.

MARCUS

What?

ELEGUA

All the years I been in somebody church
And this the first time I feel like there's a fire shut
Up in my bones.

MARCUS

I saw Ogun crying.

ELEGUA

Huh.

MARCUS

And it reminded me of this dream I keep having . . .

ELEGUA

When your daddy was little,
He run around here talking about his dreams.
And at the time . . . At the time all seem right with it.
Every now and then somebody catch the number off
Something he say but it ain't never catch hold of nothing
Serious. And then one day, one . . . huh.

MARCUS

Ms. Elegua?

ELEGUA

Go head tell me your dream.

MARCUS

All of it?

ELEGUA

Nah everything but the good part.

MARCUS

There is this man. He always in the rain . . . And he saying
   things to
Me. Light at first
Then so hard I can barely hear. Hard rain.
Rain so hard it look like it's coming from the
Ground it's hitting that hard. And he keep . . .
He keep telling me . . . Things . . .

ELEGUA

MARCUS

You okay?

ELEGUA

Fine. What he saying? I' th' dream, huh?

MARCUS

I on't remember when I wake up.

OGUN SIZE

(Offstage)
Aunt Elegua!

ELEGUA

Elegua straightens up.
You ain't never seen him before?

MARCUS

No.

ELEGUA

And he ain't trying to freak you like you like it?

MARCUS

No.

ELEGUA

You want him to?

MARCUS

Maybe.

ELEGUA

Huh.

MARCUS

What?

ELEGUA

Shhh!
Keep listening to the man in your dreams.

SCENE 5

OGUN SIZE

Ogun Size enters.
Aunt Elegua!
Calling for his Aunt. Elegua!

ELEGUA

I hear you. You see I'm standing right
Here.

OGUN SIZE

Where'd you go?
Yall all right?

ELEGUA

Fine.

MARCUS

Huh.

OGUN SIZE

What you, what you two up to?

ELEGUA

Nothing.

MARCUS

Uh-uh.

OGUN SIZE

Uh-huh.

ELEGUA

We was just talking about old times.

MARCUS

Old times.

ELEGUA

I was just telling Marcus here . . .

MARCUS

She was telling me . . .

ELEGUA

How you and Oshoosi and his daddy were friends.

OGUN SIZE

I mean we wasn't friends . . .
I mean he and Shoosi were . . .

MARCUS

So you knew my daddy Ogun?

OGUN SIZE

Yeah I knew him . . . but he was . . .

ELEGUA

Close.

MARCUS

Close?

OGUN SIZE

Close to my brother . . . My brother Oshoosi.
They was . . .
Marcus how you getting home?

ELEGUA

Reckon the same way he got here!

MARCUS

What you mean "close"?

OGUN SIZE

Nothing.

ELEGUA

Swat. Eh!
You need to worry bout your ailing auntie who

Getting tapped like a natural resource by these
Lisquitos! Swat.

OGUN SIZE

Oh . . . I'm sorry Aunt Ele you ready to go.

ELEGUA

Nah I'm sitting here hitting myself 'cause I'm
Into it! C'mon here!

OGUN SIZE

You sure you don't want a ride home Marcus?

ELEGUA

Elegua shaking her head.
Let it lone now.

MARCUS

Thank you. I'ma walk.
Marcus looks to the sky.

ELEGUA

Gon head Marcus. Keep your head up.
Out the side of her mouth:
Hold to that dream.

A Mirage

MARCUS

Wanna watch while I try and put two and two
And get more than four? All I remember in that
Dream is . . . light and water and a man. And there

In the sky is the moon, and if I walk a lil further
I'll find water . . . maybe even the man
Stupid . . . No . . . shrugs. Huh. Maybe I find . . . Huh.
Marcus moves.

SCENE 6

SHAUNTA IYUN

Shaunta Iyun enters.
Marcus!
Where the hell you going?

MARCUS

Out by the waters.

SHAUNTA IYUN

Uh Marcus . . .

MARCUS

Wanna come?

SHAUNTA IYUN

It's dark!

MARCUS

So that mean, no?
Marcus moves to . . .

SHAUNTA IYUN

Wait . . . uh Marcus

MARCUS

Huh?

SHAUNTA IYUN

What star is that near the moon?

MARCUS

Venus.

SHAUNTA IYUN

Oh. And what's the closest planet to the sun?

MARCUS

Mercury.

SHAUNTA IYUN

Thanks and are you sweet?

MARCUS

What!

SHAUNTA IYUN

Damnit . . . almost.

MARCUS

Shaunta!

SHAUNTA IYUN

I let you off easy earlier but come
On now. We got to talk about this.

MARCUS

Why?

SHAUNTA IYUN

Because I wanna know.

MARCUS

Stop wanting . . .

SHAUNTA IYUN

And you need to say it.

MARCUS

Marcus looks away.

SHAUNTA IYUN

Marcus you out here at this hour wandering
Where? Near the waters?
What you trying to find? What you running
Away from?

MARCUS

I ain't running from . . .
I told you there is . . . a dream keeping me up.
I told it to Ms. Elegua and she say . . .

SHAUNTA IYUN

Wait a minute.

MARCUS

It's got all this rain in it . . .

SHAUNTA IYUN

Ms. Elegua . . .
The same lady who used to chase
Osha around the projects with a lighter
Talking bout, "I burn your choochie hairs!"

MARCUS

I know . . .

SHAUNTA IYUN

This the same lady who smell like Dewar's
White Label at communion.

MARCUS

Shaunta Iyun . . .

SHAUNTA IYUN

The same chick . . .

MARCUS

She say . . . She say my daddy used to dream too.
That his dreams meant something. Maybe
Mine do too.

SHAUNTA IYUN

What?

OBA

(Offstage)
Marcus!

MARCUS

Oh shit it's my mama!

OBA

Marcus Eshu!
Oba enters
Marcus!
Calling for her son . . .

MARCUS

Shaunta Iyun . . . ?

SHAUNTA IYUN

No.

MARCUS

Please!?!

SHAUNTA IYUN

Lord!

MARCUS

Marcus hides in the night.

SCENE 7

OBA

Hey Shaunta.

SHAUNTA IYUN

Ms. Oba how you?

OBA

Good. You seen Marcus?

SHAUNTA IYUN

Yeah.

MARCUS

OBA

Where is he?

SHAUNTA IYUN

Oh, I don't know.

OBA

I thought you said you seen him.

SHAUNTA IYUN

Earlier today, at the funeral.

OBA

Huh.

SHAUNTA IYUN

Sad funeral.

OBA

Oh yeah it was.

SHAUNTA IYUN

I mean I ain't one to cry but Shango was
Such a hero, you know? Going off to fight
That fight in Iraq.

OBA

It's true.

SHAUNTA IYUN

They say that fighting in the Middle East
Ain't neva gon stop Ms. Oba what you
Think?

OBA

Well . . .

SHAUNTA IYUN

I mean they been fighting like that since
The times of Abraham. Ain't neva been
Peace between them. You a Bible-beating
Woman you know.

OBA

Hold on Shaunta . . .

SHAUNTA IYUN

Oh I'm sorry did I say that out loud.

OBA

Yes you did!

SHAUNTA IYUN

You know my mama raised me to speak
My mind. You raise Marcus like that?

OBA

I told Marcus . . .

SHAUNTA IYUN

'Cause he seem like he always scared to
Say how he really feel. He ever come to
You and tell you some secret about him?

OBA

Um. No. I mean not since he was a child.

SHAUNTA IYUN

But if Marcus told you something . . .
Something was hurting his heart, you would
Listen right? You would hear him.

OBA

Huh. Why you . . . you know some secret about
Marcus?

SHAUNTA IYUN

Oh. Oh no I was just asking. I mean . . . he
My best friend but he can be so secretive
Sometimes. Once he told me that he thought
Maybe he had dreams . . .

OBA

Dreams?

SHAUNTA IYUN

Yeah, yeah like his daddy.

OBA

To herself:
I wonder which dream his daddy give im.

SHAUNTA IYUN

Ma'am?

OBA

Nothing. Let me go find this boy.

SHAUNTA IYUN

So loud:
Oh All Right. You Be Careful Ms. Oba
AND IF I SEE MARCUS TONIGHT I WILL
Make sure to tell him you say, "GET
HOME NOW!"

OBA

Uh thank you . . . Shaunta. Yeah.
Oba exits.

MARCUS

Marcus nods to his friend.

SHAUNTA IYUN

She smiles.

MARCUS

Marcus exits.

SCENE 8

There is a noise heard offstage like a gunshot or loud fireworks.

SHAUNTA IYUN

Marcus!

OSHA

Enter Osha.
Walking fast.

(The sound again!)

OSHA

Her breath comes loose . . .

SHAUNTA IYUN

She holds her stomach . . .

> OSHA

She catches her knee . . .

> SHAUNTA IYUN AND OSHA

She . . .

> TERRELL

Enter Terrell laughing his ass off.
Damn what's wrong with yall.

> OSHA

Somebody out here . . .

> SHAUNTA IYUN

Shooting!

> TERRELL

Huh. And what you come out here
To do Shaunta Iyun eat him?

> OSHA

What you doing out here?

> TERRELL

Shooting fireworks.

> OSHA

That was your . . .

> SHAUNTA IYUN

Stupid ass.
What the hell you lighting fireworks for?

> OSHA

It ain't the fourth.

SHAUNTA IYUN

It's near bout September!

OSHA

Who called Marcus' name?

SHAUNTA IYUN

I did girl I thought he was here and . . .

OSHA

Don't even say it. Where he at?

SHAUNTA IYUN

Went out by the waters. Talking bout
That dream and Elegua . . . Talking crazy
Girl.

OSHA

This time a night? It's near bout
Morning! What's on his mind?

TERRELL

Probably some dick.

OSHA

Eh!

SHAUNTA IYUN

Silly nigga!

TERRELL

Osha girl, damn red, I'm saying why you
Be gay-chasing that nigga, Marcus?

OSHA

First of all . . .

TERRELL

You gon end up on *Oprah* I'm telling you.

OSHA

Marcus is just sensitive . . .

SHAUNTA IYUN

. . . And sweet.

OSHA

Right.
You wouldn't know nothing bout that . . .

SHAUNTA IYUN

Or a bath.

OSHA

Dirty butt.

TERRELL

Yall gon catch a whole lotta hell running behind
That homo.

SHAUNTA IYUN

Least we ain't gon catch the yit-yit running behind yo ass.

TERRELL

Shaunta you don't run nowhere.
If you did we all feel you coming.
Ain't that what Shaunta mean
In the Cherokee? "Girl-Who-Run-Like-Thunder"?

SHAUNTA IYUN

Osha . . .
Shaunta Iyun calls
To her friend.
Osha girl! You
Hear something?

OSHA

What?

SHAUNTA IYUN

Who?

OSHA

SHAUNTA IYUN

Shaunta feels around in the dark.
She slaps Terrell on the face.

TERRELL

Eh girl!

SHAUNTA IYUN

Oh Terrell that's yo black ass.
Damn boi you better wear bright
Colors this time of night.

TERRELL

Whatever heifer!

SHAUNTA IYUN

I'm just saying you better open
Your eyes bright or smile the one.

I lost you completely, soot. Thought
The devil was calling for me.

OSHA

Girl me too!
A gunshot is heard.

(Pah.)

TERRELL

Wasn't me.

SHAUNTA IYUN

Lord . . .

OSHA

Where you say he went?

SHAUNTA IYUN

C'mon let's go see.

TERRELL

See, that's how bitches get kilt round
Here, investigating shit. Just like the
White folks in the scary movies they
Hear the strange noise and they got to
Go deeper in the woods n shit. "No
Lil white skinny girl don't go in that
Dark basement! Hannibal, Freddy,
Jason in the cellar playing the *Carmina
Burana* haunting music with his dick
Tucked tween his legs he bout to come
For you girl, run!" Nope, she just
Standing there calling for her friend.

Terrell gives his best Jodie Foster or
Jamie Lee, "Mike, you there." She don't
Feel it till it's too late. Don't sense nothing
Till wicked man done sliced her up and through
Uh-huh. Yall go ahead and keep on
Wanting to see what's happening.
End up snoting like them white girls
In scary movies. Talking bout, "I'm so
Scared."

SHAUNTA IYUN

OSHA

SHAUNTA IYUN

You ready girl?

OSHA

Right, behind you girl.

TERRELL

Damn Osha girl da summer
Done been good to you! Lawd
Shawty! Wait up!
Terrell exits.
In pursuit of that ass.

SCENE 9

MARCUS

Marcus on Ms. Elegua's porch.
He starts to knock but . . .

ELEGUA

Hey there.

MARCUS

You heard me?

ELEGUA

You walk hard.
Think you think this a catwalk or something.

MARCUS

You always . . .

ELEGUA

Calling you out?
You need something?

MARCUS

I was headed to the waters. But I wanted to ask . . .
I don't mean to be . . .

ELEGUA

Boy stop worrying bout disrespecting folks . . . keep
That mess up see if you don't have ulcers all up and through
Your prostrate.

MARCUS

Earlier,
You were going to tell me something else.

ELEGUA

I'm tired.

MARCUS

Ma'am I know you old and prolly . . .

ELEGUA

Call me old one more 'gin.

MARCUS

Let me finish.

ELEGUA

MARCUS

I'm just confused. I mean why my daddy dreams made
You sad? What bout my dreams make you get quiet.

ELEGUA

They used to say that boys like you, with um Ralph
Tresvant Sensitivity have . . . can see things rest of us
Can't quite.

MARCUS

ELEGUA

Say sweet boys got a secret of sight.

MARCUS

I'm not . . .

ELEGUA

You marched your lil light-skin self all the way over here
To lie?

MARCUS

I mean . . . who said . . .

ELEGUA

Folks before your time.

MARCUS

Huh that's crazy.

ELEGUA

Fore my time.

MARCUS

Stch.
They ain't even have gay folks in Africa.

ELEGUA

Huh.
Don't let em fool you all your life.

MARCUS

So, my dream mean I'm . . . sweet?

ELEGUA

Gon boy . . .

MARCUS

I mean what? That's it! What about the man?

ELEGUA

I said . . .

MARCUS

And all that rain . . .

ELEGUA

GON!
Elegua trembling. Barely holding herself together.
Please . . . I don't know all. I don't. But all that rain?

Nese people round here talking bout a storm coming.
It can't mean Good. Just can't.

MARCUS

Marcus fades off her porch.

SCENE 10

SHAUNTA IYUN

STOP FOLLOWING US!

TERRELL

That ass too fat.

SHAUNTA IYUN

You know I hate you?

TERRELL

The feeling's reciprocal.

SHAUNTA IYUN

Shaunta shocked
Oh hell nah!

OSHA

Boi you learning words?

TERRELL

"Reciprocal" comes from the word "reciprocus."
"Re" meaning "back," "pro" meaning "forward."

Right now we need to "re pro" out this damn
Offroad.

OSHA

Not till we find Marcus.

TERRELL

It's dark as hell out here.
She know where she going?

SHAUNTA IYUN

Hm-huh.

TERRELL

How the hell? 'Cause she got them pretty eyes they
Can see everything.

OSHA

Oh. Hey . . . boy . . .

TERRELL

Yeah . . .
So where we wandering?

SHAUNTA IYUN

To the spot her n Marcus first kiss.

TERRELL

Euh!

OSHA

Dag Shaunta!

TERRELL

Out here?

SHAUNTA IYUN

They were nine.

OSHA

It was just a . . .

SHAUNTA IYUN

First n last.

OSHA

It was our favorite spot

SHAUNTA IYUN

Was . . .

OSHA

C'mon yall walk up.

Spirit in the Dark

MARCUS

Trust. I know. Ain't no answers out here. Not to
Me particular
Just sky and dust but ain't we all?
Don't you wish it was?
Don't you wish the days, all damn day, running into
Everything that scares the . . . Outta you would just wash
Out into the waters, drain away. That the disappointed
You strange-boy stares would light up and leave, like, not
Look down on you wondering, "What you doing?
What you thinking? What you dreaming?" Specially when
On't know yo ownself. Looking at you like you a problem
Staring at you like, "Where your shame?"
Right when everything seems simple. I might be . . .

Or at least it might be all right to be . . . here come some
    secret.
Some dream.
And you just smile and
Smile. You know that feeling? To just smile and smile and
Smile and smile and smile and smile and . . . when you wanna
Just get up on tabletops and scream you want to say, say . . . huh
Huh.
It's nice out here, you think? The Bayou. Maybe it's magic out
Here. I always thought so . . . Magic. "Secret of sight."
    More like
The . . . more like the secret of sweet. The secret is ain't
    nobody
Think it's a secret cept me, cept those who don't want to see.
And those who do keep talking bout me saying things to me
Man even my own dreams won't let me . . . these the times
You wish for a daddy, maybe not, maybe he wouldn't be
    proud of
Me . . . but at least you can scream at somebody you can . . .
    stand up
To em and tell him tell how it hurt you to be . . . say, "I ain't
Put this black skin on me I didn't press these . . . boy-boy
Thoughts into my head. You think I set out to be dreaming
    o dis
Man
Old
Enough
To be my . . . you
Talking to me slowly i' th' water n rain crying, laughing
Singing sometimes all in the rain. I didn't make him up I ain't
Conjure him to me. All I am is here
Heard, here so . . . so you don't got to understand me 'cause
    I don't

I don't hardly either just . . . just love me."
You ever wish it would all just wash away?
Never heard
A black boy say that I bet. Not out loud.
Wish them waters would
Rise up like that water and take it all, me too, out and away.
    You
Wish that sometimes? I do. I do.

SCENE 11

OGUN SIZE

Be careful what you wish for Marcus.
Enter Ogun Size.

MARCUS

Marcus moves.

OGUN SIZE

Where you going?

MARCUS

I don't know.

OGUN SIZE

I hope not closer out there to that water.

MARCUS

Nah . . . I can't even swim.

OGUN SIZE

Laughing.
Me neither. So we both be outta luck.

MARCUS

What you doing out here?

OGUN SIZE

Good evening to you too.

MARCUS

I'm sorry I mean how you . . .

OGUN SIZE

Nah, you ain't got to apologize . . .
Something caught in your eye Marcus.
Ogun wipes a tear.

MARCUS

Thank you.

OGUN SIZE

You ain't all right so what ailing you?

MARCUS

Been one of them days.

OGUN SIZE

I hear you man. Three times a charm they say.
Third time I done put down somebody who ought
To be burying me. Three times of saying good-bye.
When your daddy died . . .

MARCUS

Why everybody do that?
Stop up like when they coming to tell me about . . .

OGUN SIZE

You know folks, me too, you trying to explain something
You ain't never really understood. You shut up for fear of
    putting
It wrong.

MARCUS

Was he . . . sweet?

OGUN SIZE

He could be.

MARCUS

No I mean—

OGUN SIZE

Interrupting.
But he could be as mean as the devil too. Like every man
We all got the ability of being a lot, but you seeing that,
Sure.

MARCUS

Huh.

OGUN SIZE

Sit a while, hause.

MARCUS

All right.

OGUN SIZE

You a lot like them: my brother, your daddy.
Feel everything don't you? I ain't felt nothing till I

Saw you standing there staring at me at that
Funeral today.

OGUN SIZE

MARCUS

You saw me?

OGUN SIZE

Felt like the world push up to my feet.

MARCUS

You mean come from under . . .

OGUN SIZE

No I mean I finally felt the ground.

MARCUS

OGUN SIZE

Memories, right they wash over you out here.

MARCUS

Where's your brother now, Ogun?

OGUN SIZE

Situation happened with him and
Your daddy; they got in trouble good with the
Law and
Um well I . . . It was me who . . . I asked him . . .
To leave town. Told him
He better if he left. Nigga never listen to
A word I say. Why he start that day I never
Know. Your daddy . . . he turned hisself in.
Walked hisself right into jail one day. Guess
Without . . . Without Oshoosi . . .

MARCUS

And that's where he died.

OGUN SIZE

Yeah that's where they say Legba died. In jail.
But he wasn't the same after Oshoosi left.
They was always together those t . . .

MARCUS

Please don't . . . just tell me about them.

OGUN SIZE

They . . . huh . . . it's hard to tell. 'Cause they . . .
They was always made some people uncomfortable
I can't lie make my stomach funny talking bout it . . .
But some people in this world they just fit right.
. . . My brother couldn't never sleep . . . he always had bad
  dreams.
Used to piss me off. Waking up dreaming
Crying, wanting to stay up. Got so I started ignoring him.
  I would
Hear him awake and act like I'm sleep or something. Act like
I ain't paying attention. One night Legba your daddy was
  spending
The night over, they was bout your age. Shoosi wake up
  crying.
I thought he gon embarrass hisself crying in front of
  company.
I heard Elegba say I heard him say whisper, "Shhh! Shhh!
  It's gon be
Okay. Shhh, now, Oshoosi it's gon be all right."
And he stop crying. I heard him not saying anything.
And I turned over to see what they was doing. See what he
  had done to make

Him stop. And Elegba had done hugged Oshoosi
Close and they had laid back down again.
I didn't know what to say. Still don't.
The next morning, I say, "You two niggas get yall ass up."
Huh.
I was mad.

MARCUS

Why?

OGUN SIZE

All my life I tried to get my brother to quit crying and
Sleep like that and never could. Never could.

MARCUS

You got something in your eye, Ogun.
Marcus wipes a tear.

OGUN SIZE

Look at us both out here crying.

MARCUS

Least we crying together stead of separate.
He smiles.

OGUN SIZE

MARCUS

He don't know why?

OGUN SIZE

He smiles back.

OGUN SIZE AND MARCUS

He . . .

SCENE 12

TERRELL

Oh yall niggas gay!
Enter Terrell.

OSHA

With Osha girl.

SHAUNTA IYUN

And Shaunta Iyun.

TERRELL

They was kissing!

SHAUNTA IYUN

Shut up . . .
Mr. Ogun.

MARCUS

Wait . . .

SHAUNTA IYUN

You gay?

OGUN SIZE

Laughing.
No . . . I'm too old to be gay . . .

SHAUNTA IYUN

You was kissing!

MARCUS

Marcus braving.
I kissed him.

OGUN SIZE

Too sad to be gay . . .

OSHA

You what?

OGUN SIZE

Too . . .

TERRELL

He sweet . . .

MARCUS

Shut up . . .

TERRELL

You gay . . . what . . .
Ray Charles can see that
And he blind and dead.

SHAUNTA IYUN

And you couldn't tell me . . .

MARCUS

Osha . . .

OSHA

You know I love you?

MARCUS

Marcus stung.
I love you . . .

SHAUNTA IYUN

But like a friend.

OSHA

Osha's face . . .

SHAUNTA IYUN

Falls into the water.

OSHA

Exit Osha.

OGUN SIZE

I'm sorry Marcus.

TERRELL

Yall finna kiss again?

SHAUNTA IYUN, MARCUS AND OGUN SIZE

SHUT UP!

OSHA

Enter Osha.
Marcus!
Calling for her friend.
Marcus Eshu!
Do you know how many niggas would
Stomp a hole in Heaven to get with me?
You telling me you rather be with him?

OGUN SIZE

No!

OSHA

Gay or no he old and I'm phyne!

TERRELL

Yes Lord.

OSHA

They all stare at Terrell.

TERRELL

To himself,
"Shut. Up."

OSHA

Marcus be my friend.

MARCUS

I am . . .

OSHA

Tell me the truth.

MARCUS

I do.

OSHA

Them dreams you was talking bout before . . .
They about a man, huh.

MARCUS

Yes but he . . .

OSHA

You ain't dreaming about me.

MARCUS

No, Osha girl. I don't need you
In my dreams. You my friend in
Life.

OSHA

I wouldn't be so quick on that one Marc . . .
Eh boy walk me home.

MARCUS

Osha . . .

OSHA

Don't call my name . . . Don't call my name . . .
Don't call me . . . Don't . . . Don't.
Osha exits.

TERRELL

Followed by Terrell.

SHAUNTA IYUN

And Shaunta Iyun too.

A Vision on the Waters

OGUN SIZE

Quiet now Marcus.

MARCUS

I hear it Ogun. I hear it.
Marcus moves.

OGUN SIZE

Night.

MARCUS

Night.

OGUN SIZE

Hey . . .

MARCUS

Hmm.

OGUN SIZE

What was you and Elegua talking bout earlier?
Was you really talking bout old times?

MARCUS SIZE

I told her . . . I told her a dream I had.

OGUN SIZE

Huh. Tell it to me. Tell me your dream.

MARCUS

Marcus stares.
There's this man . . . and all this rain.

(Lights shift to Oshoosi Size standing in rain. Humming.)

ACT 2

SCENE 1

OBA

(Offstage)
Marcus Eshu!
I really do believe you must've lost
Your true mind boy! Or smacked your
Forehead on the pavement!

MARCUS

Marcus Eshu sits in his room watching
The walls.

OBA

(Offstage)
I don't
Care how upset you were or what you
Were looking to find, you don't bring

Your behind in here drifting like the
Morning dew talking bout some . . .

MARCUS

He is on punishment for coming home
So late the other night. He tried to
Explain to his mother what had happened . . .

OBA

(Offstage)
Shut Up!

MARCUS

She was having none of that.

OBA

What were you thinking, boy?
Enter Oba.
You know how many boys your age get
Shot or throwed up in jail round here for
Just walking? Huh? Do you? Answer me!

MARCUS

I . . .

OBA

Shut up!
Sitting round here walking the
Streets like your daddy! You wanna know
About your daddy he used to walk around
Too and look what happened to him. Dead
And in the ground. You want that do you?

MARCUS

Tears in her eyes . . .

OBA

You scared the daylights outta me round
Here being fast and grown!
There's a storm on the way!
What were you
Thinking? What did I ever do to make you . . .

MARCUS

Mama . . .

OBA

No! I don't wanna hear nothing
Out you. I means that Marcus Eshu I do.
Lord God help me . . .
Oba exits. Talking to the Father.

SCENE 2

MARCUS

Marcus sits in his room staring at the afternoon
Light.

SHAUNTA IYUN

Marcus!
Shaunta Iyun enters
Whispering Loud for her friend
Marcus Eshu!

MARCUS

Shaunta what you doing out there girl?

SHAUNTA IYUN

I'm doing the Jenny Craig "Call and
Response" workout plan. What it look like I'm
Doing. I'm freeing you like they did
Stephen Biko.

MARCUS

Didn't Stephen Biko die in jail?

SHAUNTA IYUN

Nigga sneak out the house!

MARCUS

I'm on punishment.

SHAUNTA IYUN

Thus I said "sneak."
C'mon I gotta talk to you about something . . .

MARCUS

I am in enough trouble
As it is. I am not going nowhere with . . .

SHAUNTA IYUN

Ooh you cranky what's wrong with you?

MARCUS

Gon Shaunta I'm tired.

SHAUNTA IYUN

You ain't been sleeping?

MARCUS

Trying not to.

SHAUNTA IYUN

'Cause of the . . .
Huh.
What . . . what happens in that dream?

MARCUS

Nah, last time I went around talking about
What was in my head I ended up wet, tired
And locked in here. Done
Speaking my mind for a lil while now . . .

SHAUNTA IYUN

But Marcus the rain . . .

MARCUS

Shaunta . . .

(Elegua is offstage, singing.)

MARCUS

Marcus hears it.

SHAUNTA IYUN

How could he not?

(Elegua is offstage, singing.)

MARCUS

What's that?

ELEGUA

Enter Elegua
Hair undone. Bent low to the ground . . .

MARCUS

Singing?

SHAUNTA IYUN

Almost screaming.

(Elegua sings.)

MARCUS

What's wrong with her, Shaunta?

SHAUNTA IYUN

Swhat I was trying to tell you. A storm coming.
Ogun sending Elegua away. Say, she don't need
To be out this close to the waters. Say, she can
Come back when it's over.

MARCUS

What she walking around screaming for?

SHAUNTA IYUN

She won't say . . . She won't talk about it with
Nobody but ever since you told her about that Dream she
Been wandering around crying out like
That. Going on some days now.
She looks to Marcus . . .

MARCUS

Me? I didn't tell her nothing except . . .

(Elegua sings.)

ELEGUA

Elegua exits.

SHAUNTA IYUN

MARCUS

It was just some stupid flick in my forehead.
It wasn't nothing to scream about.

SHAUNTA IYUN

Who you trying to convince?
Don't stay locked up in there forever.

MARCUS

Where you going Shaunta Iyun?

SHAUNTA IYUN

To make sure she get home safe.
Shaunta Iyun exits.

SCENE 3

MARCUS

Marcus stares after his friend . . .

SHUA

(Offstage)
Damn you got pretty eyes for a nigga.

MARCUS

Marcus stunned . . .

SHUA

Enter Shua with his Kangol
Low . . . Down low.
I mean I'm saying though son the way the
Light playing on your eyes or whatnot, that's
What's up though.

MARCUS

Oh . . . thank you.

SHUA

So, yo son what you on?

MARCUS

Oh, I don't do drugs man.

SHUA

Word? Are you serious son? You think . . .
Huh. Country niggas. Yo, I'm trying to
Say yo, you get down?

MARCUS

Where?

SHUA

With dudes, son!

MARCUS

Oh . . . oh . . . Oh! I mean . . .
Oh. Why?

SHUA

Why else I'ma be asking you?
Come outside.

MARCUS

I . . . Right now?

SHUA

What, you want the dick later?

MARCUS

I . . . um . . . oh . . .
Laughing.
My mama . . .

SHUA

Oh your daddy coming too?

MARCUS

My daddy's dead.

SHUA

Damn yo! You said that and it was like
"Flame on" in your eyes, son, when you
Talk about your old mans. No disrespect famo.

MARCUS

What?

SHUA

My condolences . . .

MARCUS

Thank you . . .

SHUA

How long he been dead for?

MARCUS

I barely know'd the nig . . .

SHUA

Now don't get sad man. Now the light
Almost gone out your eyes. You want,
If it keep them eyes bright, I let you call
Me Daddy.

MARCUS

Stupid . . .

SHUA

Serious, man.
He smiles.
Come outside.

MARCUS

I can't . . .

SHUA

Oh aight.
Shua turns to leave . . .

MARCUS

Wait . . . Meet me. Out by the waters,
The Bayou.

SHUA

The swamp?

MARCUS

Yeah right off Buras Drive.

SHUA

How I'ma find you, the light in your eyes?

MARCUS

Blush.
Yeah something . . . something like
That. I'm Marcus . . . What's your . . .

SHUA

Daddy, remember? Call me Daddy.

SCENE 4

MARCUS

Marcus Eshu, sneaking out in the late.

OGUN SIZE

Eh Marcus . . .
Enter Ogun Size.

MARCUS

What you doin out here?

OGUN SIZE

How you doin?

MARCUS

Oh . . . how you doing?

OGUN SIZE

I'm all right. Boy time you try to put things
Down and you know plant yourself you gotta

Pick up and go . . . I'm trying to send Elegua
Off you know.

MARCUS

Uh-huh.

OGUN SIZE

She keep on wandering off . . . She ain't slick
I know she ain't "senile" yet.

MARCUS

Nope.

OGUN SIZE

Say the storm
Might do make landfall. You never know
This woman done wandered . . .
You haven't seen her?

MARCUS

No.

OGUN SIZE

I haven't seen you.

MARCUS

Been on punishment.

OGUN SIZE

What you doing out?

MARCUS

Going to meet a friend.

OGUN SIZE

Oh you . . .

MARCUS

A new friend . . .

OGUN SIZE

Oh. Oh!

MARCUS

Smiles.

OGUN SIZE

Well I gotta find Elegua. Listen man, she
Been acting strange ever since . . .

MARCUS

Yeah I heard.

OGUN SIZE

Can you tell the Dream again maybe I can . . .

MARCUS

I don't remember, I haven't had it . . .

OGUN SIZE

The rain in it, is it bad?

MARCUS

Yeah it gets pretty bad.

OGUN SIZE

Like bad, bad . . .

MARCUS

Bad.
To himself, "Bad nigga."

OGUN SIZE

And the man in it?

MARCUS

Yeah . . .

OGUN SIZE

What does he look like?

MARCUS

I gotta go . . .

OGUN SIZE

Eh, didn't you just say you was on punishment?
Your mama know . . .

MARCUS

Ogun you ain't my daddy man. I mean . . . You know
You ain't my daddy, I ain't your brother so just . . .
Gon find your aunt, Ogun. I gotta go.
Marcus exits.

SCENE 5

SHUA

Night.

MARCUS

Sittin watching the waters.

                    SHUA
Shua with his cap covering his
Eyes.

                    MARCUS
Marcus with his hands in his lap.

                    SHUA
Shua kisses his teeth.
Stch!
How old are you?

                    MARCUS
Sixteen . . . I just turned sixteen. You?

                    SHUA
Twenty . . . two.

                    MARCUS

                    SHUA

                    MARCUS
Crickets.

                    SHUA
Shifting.

                    MARCUS
Huh.

                    SHUA
Whatever.

327

MARCUS

Crickets.

SHUA

Shua kisses his teeth.
Stch . . .
So wassup man?

MARCUS

Nothing.

SHUA

I see that. Yo, where you from?

MARCUS

From here.

SHUA

Yeah you seem like you from down
Here. Country niggas.
Ey shorty yall get storms round
Here? I was up on the news yo
Say it's one coming.

MARCUS

Sometimes . . . Yeah.

SHUA

Damn yo this my first time down
Here. Visiting my peoples.

MARCUS

So you're from up North?

SHUA

From the boogie down baby.

MARCUS

That's the Bronx right?

SHUA

Uh-huh.
Shua looks over Marcus.
Marcus in his jeans lookin just right.
You aight.

MARCUS

Thanks.

SHUA

Yeah you all right. Got a lil phatty
Or what not . . .

MARCUS

Thanks . . .

SHUA

Them eyes sexy . . .

MARCUS

Marcus bites his lips.

SHUA

Sex lips too . . . Sexy-
Ass lips.

MARCUS

Black boy blushing.

SHUA

C'mere . . .

MARCUS

Marcus moves.

SHUA

You gonna call me Daddy, Eyes?
Shua puts his fingers to Marcus' lips.

MARCUS

Marcus kisses Shua's fingers.

SHUA

Shua moves his hand behind Marcus' head.

MARCUS

He pulls Marcus' head down toward
His lap.

SHUA

Lights.

SCENE 6

OSHA

Osha stomps onto her porch.
Lord . . .

SHUN

Shun walking up . . .
Every night, Osha?

OSHA

I'm just spending
Time with him while I can.

SHUN

I understand girl I'm just saying give
Him some time to miss you. You young
Chicks don't know how to tether niggas.

OSHA

He'll miss me when he's gone back
To the Bronx.

SHUN

You need to get him to help put up my storm
Boards messing round here talking bout some, "Hanging
Out." Oh chile never mind. He from up there he
Don't know nothing bout no shutters.
I don't trust them niggas from up there no how.

OSHA

You rather me be hanging with Marcus
Still?

SHUN

I didn't mind you . . . hanging with that boy.
I just tried to tell you he was his way, like
That. You know I don't hate on the gays.

OSHA

Mama just go in the house.

SHUN

Oh hell nah! Get your ass in this house
He can come ring the doorbell like normal bastards.

OSHA

Mama please just let me wait for him by myself.

SHUN

Huh. You get yo ass in this house come late night.
I don't care whicha way a hurricane coming, you
Got school tomorrow. Hear me Osha girl?

OSHA

I hear you.

SHUN

Shun goes into the house, talking trash:
Boy come down here talking all side
Ways. He better just be courting and
Not trying to do the electric slide with
My baby I'll light his ass up. I mean that . . .

SCENE 7

MARCUS

Enter Marcus Eshu.
She all right?

OSHA

You know how she get.

MARCUS

How you?

OSHA

All right.

MARCUS

You busy or something

OSHA

Waiting for a friend . . .

MARCUS

Who? Like . . . like a new friend?
Smiles.

OSHA

What it matter to you?

MARCUS

I ain't come here to fight.

OSHA

What you come for?

MARCUS

I met a . . . a friend too. I wanted to
Tell you.

OSHA

Ehuh! Tell Shaunta Iyun she like to hear
That kind of stuff.

MARCUS

Last time I checked you my best too.

OSHA

Yeah I thought so too tell I figured out
You was lying.

MARCUS

Lying!

OSHA

I didn't stutter man. Lied. You knew Marcus,
Say you didn't. How I was feeling? How
You gon be my best friend and not tell me?
Huh?

MARCUS

I . . .

OSHA

All you got for me Marcus Eshu? "I."

MARCUS

Marcus laughs.
Eh girl, tell me how you didn't
Know I wasn't interested? Huh? Tell me how you
Couldn't tell after all the years after all the teasing
And the fights . . . the time you punched Eric down
The way in the stomach 'cause he called me a faggot?

OSHA

Huh.
Osha laughs.

MARCUS

He still be running when he see
You coming talking bout some "gone girl."
When we would play "hide and go get it" with the
Other kids. Everybody round us hunching and I'm
Talking bout some "let's play cuddle."

OSHA

I just thought you was being romantic.

MARCUS

Girl!

OSHA

All right. All right . . . I shoulda've known.
I mean you the only one I could sing *The Wiz*
Straight through with.

(Marcus sings.
Osha sings.
Marcus and Osha sing.)

SHUA

Enter Shua
Kangol pulled
Way down.

MARCUS AND OSHA

Hey.

MARCUS

OSHA

SHUA

OSHA

You know Joshua?

MARCUS

Joshua?

OSHA

Osha turns to Marcus.
You met before?

SHUA

Shua puts his fingers to his lips.
To Osha:
You ready to go?

MARCUS

Huh.

OSHA

We'll talk later Marcus.

SCENE 8

OBA

Oba on the porch.
I didn't go looking for you 'cause I didn't want to
Know really where you was. I didn't call for you
For fear that you might hear me and not answer
Back.

MARCUS

OBA

I ain't got much to say either Marcus but hear me
Out. You disobeyed me. The first time you just didn't
Tell me but this time you heard what I said and still
You went on your own way. Made your own path.

MARCUS

OBA

I just want to know where it's leading you?
This sneaking and secrets and lying, and making a
Fool of . . . did you really think I didn't know that thick
Girl was hiding you the other night? Where is it
Taking you, Marcus Eshu? You turning into the man
You want to be? Or the man you need to be? Or . . .
No matter what you like, or don't, you still a man.
All men have to be men. They say a woman can't
Teach you that . . . I got news for you, no man can
Either. Only you can learn it for you.

MARCUS

OBA

Gon on in there and lay down . . . if you want. I
Can't make you do much a nothing these days.
I figured I would just offer.

MARCUS

Marcus moves to . . .

OBA

What's this Dream I hear you got going?

MARCUS

Ma'am?

OBA

Is it something I could . . . wanna hear?

> MARCUS

It's something I barely remember.

> OBA

Night.

> MARCUS

Night.

A Dream of Drag

> MARCUS

That night.
Marcus is
Sleeping dreaming this very . . . odd, weird dream.
Not the one . . . no this other mess.
In this dream are the very best friends
Shaunta Iyun and Osha girl.
All Caught in a Sun Shower.
To the best:
It's raining.

> OSHA

We see that Marcus.

> MARCUS

But the sun's out.

> SHAUNTA IYUN

I see why they put you in the advanced
Class Marcus.

> OSHA

Them good observation skills.

MARCUS

Why yall being so mean!

SHAUNTA IYUN

It's raining.

OSHA

And you should have told us.

MARCUS

I didn't know.

OSHA

Course you did.

SHAUNTA IYUN

It was raining in your dream.

MARCUS

Lord first I couldn't get nobody to listen to that
Stupid dream. Now everybody acting like it King's
Dream. Look . . .
I knew it was raining hard in the dream
But this ain't that. This a sun shower
You know what we used to do in a sun
Shower. Osha, Shaunta Iyun.

SHAUNTA IYUN AND OSHA

Rain . . .

MARCUS

Shaunta Iyun going in.
Osha struggling . . .

> OSHA

Hey!
Ain't we too old to be playing this game.

> MARCUS

Shaunta Iyun giggling . . .

> SHAUNTA IYUN

This your Dreaming Marcus Eshu tell us.

> MARCUS

The song "Sunshower" by Dr. Buzzard's
Original Savannah Band begins to play . . .

> OSHA

Laughing
Oh hell to nah.

> SHAUNTA IYUN

We are not . . .

> MARCUS

Yes we are . . .
Shaunta pats her weave.

> OSHA

Are you . . .

> SHAUNTA IYUN

For real?

> OSHA

This was cute when we were kids Marcus.

MARCUS

Osha rocks back on her heels.

OSHA

But we grown now . . .

MARCUS

She puts her hand on her hip.

SHAUNTA IYUN

Back then they would call it kids being
Cute.

OSHA

When you grown

SHAUNTA IYUN

They call it a drag show.

MARCUS

It's my Dream. We gon do what I want.
All laughing and playing in the rain.

SHAUNTA IYUN

Ha! So you Dream of drag now?

MARCUS

Maybe guess we have to wait and see.

OSHA

Lord you are so free and easy in your Dreams
Marcus Eshu.

MARCUS

Nah not always only when I'm with you
Two . . .

MARCUS, SHAUNTA IYUN AND OSHA

My best.

MARCUS

C'mon yall sing the song.

(Marcus, Shaunta Iyun and Osha sing "Sunshower.")

MARCUS

Osha singing lead.

(Osha sings.)

MARCUS

Madam Iyun.

(Shaunta Iyun sings. Then Marcus and Osha join her.)

MARCUS

Taking over.

(Marcus sings.)

OSHA AND SHAUNTA IYUN

Sang Marcus Eshu.

(Shua enters.)

SHUA

MARCUS

The music stops. We stop dancing.
What you want?

SHUA

MARCUS

Rain pours . . . the sun is
Gone.
My friends are gone. To Shua:
Get out of my Dream.
Shua smiles.
Shua takes off his Kangol. He strips down
And now he looks like . . .

OSHOOSI SIZE

Oshoosi Size dressed in all white . . .
Shh! Shh! It's gon be okay.
Shh now Marcus. It's gon be all right . . .
Just ask him ask my brotha . . .
For me.

SCENE 9

MARCUS

The next morning
Black boy running . . .
Mama?

OBA

Oba still on the porch.

MARCUS

Mama?

OBA

MARCUS

Mama I . . . I will be right back. I have to tell
Osha and Shaunta . . .

OBA

Do what you please, Marcus.

MARCUS

I will be right back.

OBA

What you please.

MARCUS

When I come back let me in.

OBA

She goes in.

MARCUS

He runs out.

SCENE 10

SHAUNTA IYUN

Enter Shaunta Iyun eating a sandwich singing.

(Shaunta Iyun sings.)

MARCUS

Thank you Father! Shaunta.

SHAUNTA IYUN

Boy what you doing? What's wrong you coming
Round the corner breathing like the big girls?

MARCUS

Shaunta I gotta tell you something . . .

SHAUNTA IYUN

Oh now you ready to tell me something.
Wait a Dream?

MARCUS

No . . . well yeah.

SHAUNTA IYUN

It's about me and Jason Witt?

MARCUS

What?

SHAUNTA IYUN

Shaunta braving.
I know! I know! I should have told you . . .
But it's hard to come out and be like, "I like, have
Loved this *white* boy since the third grade!"

MARCUS

Shaunta Iyun.

SHAUNTA IYUN

But he so cute and nice and country as hell . . .

MARCUS

I sucked Shua's dick.

SHAUNTA IYUN

Shaunta Iyun drops her sandwich.

SHAUNTA IYUN

MARCUS

SHAUNTA IYUN

Shua?

MARCUS

Yes.

SHAUNTA IYUN

Josh-shua . . .

MARCUS

Nods.

SHAUNTA IYUN

That fake-ass neyo kat with the Usher hat?
Shaunta Iyun swats her foolish friend.
The one that Osha seeing!

MARCUS

Eh girl!

SHAUNTA IYUN

What you suck his dick for! All the
Dick in the world and you gotta suck
His!

MARCUS

Ain't like I knew she was dating him. She
And me weren't talking and his ass ain't say shit
Cept yeah that feel good.

SHAUNTA IYUN

Least you know you good at it.

MARCUS

Shaunta!

SHAUNTA IYUN

Identify your strengths

MARCUS

We gotta tell her.

SHAUNTA IYUN

We!

MARCUS

We just gon let him keep lying to her?

SHAUNTA IYUN

Uh-uh oh no ma'am. I don't like how you got Creole all the
    sudden
Marcus E. Throwing all this here *we* in the soup. *We*
Didn't give the king of New York some face. *We*
Weren't there to watch it and now *we* gon act like
We don't know nothing bout it.
Starting right, Shaunta looks
At her imaginary watch now.

MARCUS

Shaunta Iyun . . .

SHAUNTA IYUN

Eh there Marcus E. Baby BABY! What's going on man
How's that secret of sweet coming? I don't know nothing
    about
No homoerotic fellatio. Nope. Not me.
Couldn't be! Then who!

MARCUS

You right no sense in her killing us both.

SHAUNTA IYUN

Tell her you didn't mean to suck it.

MARCUS

A realization.
Just bring her out by the waters?

SHAUNTA IYUN

What?

MARCUS

Yeah just bring her out there.

SHAUNTA IYUN

Huh.
There goes a brave man.
Shaunta Iyun exits.
Damn boy made me drop my sandwich.

A Re-Collection

MARCUS

I'm old enough to know better. To know. What did
I expect to happen, did you see this coming? Huh, you
    couldn'ta . . .
Guess I wouldn't've listened or heard but
I hear now. Yessuh. I do. I hear you can't just wake up one
    morning
A Dream on your mind, in your heart, spend that day
No matter whose wedding or funeral running round
Telling everybody bout it. Just talking I got a Dream
It went like this . . . I got this feeling feels like this . . .
Lesson: When you thought about it
Prayed about it and you can't keep it to yourself . . .
Maybe it's better to run or walk away but don't give
It unto the air.
You realize that your Dreams too heavy for
Everyone else? You can grin; you can bare em but the world
Seem to light a fire or drown deep when you mention
Your innermost thoughts, wishes, desire . . . so what's that
    teaching: Keep it
To yourself? That ain't right either.
So how do you play it?
How does this run out? 'Cause right now I'm back out here
By the waters knowing more than I did, understanding
. . . Well I'm still standing but just barely
My best friend's bout to hate me, if she don't still . . . already.
Got a ol lady say she see a storm somehow in my Dream and
A mama who barely can look me in the eye 'cause she
    think I'm
On the ho stroll and she ain't but half wrong, she ain't but
    half wrong

'Cause I'm out here again waiting under the good God's sky
   for some Up
North down-low Negro and . . .
These Dreams.
All I got are these Dreams and Memories. The Dream of a
   man who
I think . . . well I know . . . but how to tell that part? How to
   explain that . . .
Stop thinking Marcus just tell him.
'Cause all that thinking this thinking ain't gon undo
Redo make do nothing. Time to quit thinking or quicker
   think so
The next move is made before the thought. The next move
   don't
Take a whole lot of thought. The next move . . . Here he
   comes.
Here we go.
Marcus moves.

SCENE 11

SHUA

Enter Shua.
Kangol: Low.
You know. Sup yo?

MARCUS

Heavy breath . . .
Hey.

SHUA

Evening, as yall say.

MARCUS

Huh that's funny, you funny, you
Always been funny?

SHUA

You all right man?

MARCUS

Oh I'm fine. Yeah I mean
Sexy: I'm fine.

SHUA

Laughing. Yeah all right.
What you stepping up?

MARCUS

Yeah I am . . . yo.

SHUA

Huh.

MARCUS

You . . . you like that?

SHUA

Your girl know what went down
Between us?

MARCUS

Uh-uh.

SHUA

So what you trying to keep this going
On the side, right?

MARCUS

Um . . . yeah.

SHUA

That's what's . . .

MARCUS

I mean no . . .
Marlene Dietrich:
I think I might be the jealous type.

SHUA

Like that? You get green . . .

MARCUS

Lauren Bacall:
Yeah, I like to keep my friends to myself.

SHUA

Shit that's cool n th gang baby.
I mean long as you can keep a secret.

MARCUS

(To us)
Is he for real?
Yeah I'm good at keeping my mouth shut.
People round here don't even know about me.

SHUA

Ha! Oh yeah?

MARCUS

Yeah . . .

SHUA

Well this time we ain't got to worry about your mouth.

MARCUS

Huh?

SHUA

I on't need your lips.

MARCUS

What you doing?

SHUA

I bet you tight.

MARCUS

Hol up . . .

SHUA

Touch.

MARCUS

Eh man!

SHUA

That's it. That's them eyes lightning up.

MARCUS

Just back up . . .

SHUA

Touch,
You making me hot, son.

MARCUS

Please . . .

SHUA

You give good ass?

MARCUS

I ain't never . . . Gon man!

SHUA

GRAB!
Can't.
Your eyes calling me.
Shua moves to . . .

MARCUS

Get off me!

(*They struggle.*
Enter Shaunta Iyun pulling Osha.)

SHAUNTA IYUN

C'mon

OSHA

Stop girl . . .

SHUA

C'mon let me get that ass nigga!

OSHA

Joshua get your hands off him!

SHUA

Shua stops.
Realizing.
Oh so yall kats trying to play me. Put my
Business out there like that? Trying to put
My shit on blast . . .

SHAUNTA IYUN

Nah you trying to put your shit on boys did that!

SHUA

Shut the fuck up . . .

MARCUS

Marcus moves.
Uh.

(He punches Shua.)

OSHA

Osha steps between.
Gon Joshua, just gon.

SHUA

Shua holding his face.
Fuck this . . . Fuck this . . .
Exit Shua.

MARCUS

Osha . . .

OSHA

What?

MARCUS

I wanted to . . . wanted to tell you.

OSHA

You told me . . .

MARCUS

I'm . . . I'm sorry.

OSHA

Me too.

MARCUS

I love you.

OSHA

Me too.
Osha exits.

MARCUS

Tears . . .

SHAUNTA IYUN

Roll down his face.
Marcus?

MARCUS

Hm?

SHAUNTA IYUN

You ain't crying 'cause she left huh?

(He shakes his head.)

SHAUNTA IYUN

You crying 'cause punching that boy
Hurt your damn hand.

(He nods.)

SHAUNTA IYUN

Laughing. Awww. Shhh! Shhh! It's gon be
Okay. Shhh now Marcus it's gon be all right . . .

MARCUS

Marcus steps back.

SHAUNTA IYUN

Like he just heard a ghost.

MARCUS

Or remembered a . . .

EPILOGUE

MARCUS

Marcus stands on Elegua's porch wanting to
Knock but her windows are all boarded-up.

OGUN SIZE

(Offstage)
She ain't home.
Enter Ogun Size.
She left to Houston finally. Be back
When the storm passes.
Ogun Size turns
To go.

MARCUS

You know dreams, Ogun?

OGUN SIZE

Ogun stops.

MARCUS

I have this dream.

OGUN SIZE

I know your dream.

MARCUS

But I didn't tell it right before.

OGUN SIZE

You got it right this time?

MARCUS

In this dream is your brother, Ogun . . .
It's your brother comes to me in this dream.
At first I didn't know . . . What, how to tell you?
But it's him come to me,
And he tell me to say, remind you,
Ask my brother . . .

(From offstage Oshoosi Size's voice merges with Marcus's.)

MARCUS AND OSHOOSI SIZE

Ask my brother Ogun.

OSHOOSI SIZE

Enter Oshoosi Size.
Tell him that it
Was better that I left. I'm better.
Gon and seen all of this world that

I could see. See a storm on its way,
Seen some rain, seen me.
But ask if he remember me
Ask if he remember . . .

MARCUS AND OSHOOSI SIZE

Ask.

OGUN SIZE

Father . . .

MARCUS

You believe, Ogun?

OGUN SIZE

No choice but to . . .

MARCUS

What it mean, Ogun? What my dream mean?

OGUN SIZE

Ogun Size can't help hearing all that Marcus
Eshu say.

MARCUS

He looks to the sky.

OGUN SIZE

Finds all the answers there. It means . . .
It means my brother's dead.
You dream like your daddy
And I'm . . . I'm tired
Just now.

MARCUS

Ogun Size marches a funeral processional by himself

OGUN SIZE

Walk with me Lord . . .
Walk with me . . .
Walk with me Lord . . .
Walk with me . . .

(Ogun Size walks in a mock processional all his own.)

MARCUS

Marcus stares after Ogun
To make sure he gets home safe.
End of play.

TARELL ALVIN MCCRANEY's plays include *The Brother/Sister Plays: In the Red and Brown Water* (winner of the 2007 Kendeda Graduate Playwriting Award), *The Brothers Size* (nominated for an Olivier Award for Outstanding Achievement by an Affiliate Theatre for London's Young Vic production) and *Marcus; Or the Secret of Sweet. The Brother/Sister* trilogy was first performed at the McCarter Theatre Center in Princeton, and then at The Public Theater in New York City. Subsequently, the trilogy has had a long run at Steppenwolf Theatre Company in Chicago.

Other plays include: *The Breach* (Southern Repertory Theater, New Orleans; Seattle Repertory Theater); *Wig Out!* (The Sundance Theatre Lab, Park City; the Royal Court Theatre, London; Vineyard Theatre, New York City);

Without/Sin (Yale Cabaret, New Haven); *Run Mourner, Run* (Yale Cabaret); *A Taurian Tale* (The 52nd Street Project, New York City) and *Promise Not to Tell* (New World School of the Arts Playwrights Festival, Miami).

Tarell was born and raised in Liberty City, the inner city area of Miami. He graduated from the New World School of the Arts High School, with the Exemplary Artist Award and the Dean's Award in Theater in 1999; matriculated into The Theatre School at DePaul University in Chicago, graduating with the Sarah Siddons Award and a BFA in Acting in 2003. He attended the British American Drama Academy (BADA) Midsummer at Oxford, studying Shakespeare with master actors and teachers from the Royal Shakespeare Company and the throughout the UK. He received his MFA in playwriting from the Yale School of Drama in 2007, being honored with the Cole Porter Playwriting Award upon graduation.

Tarell was honored with the 2007 Paula Vogel Playwriting Award from the Vineyard Theatre, and a 2007 Whiting Writers' Award. In 2008, he was awarded a Hodder Fellowship at the Lewis Center for the Arts at Princeton University. He is the International Playwright in Residence for the Royal Shakespeare Company 2008–2010, a member of New Dramatists and a member of Teo Castellanos/D-Projects in Miami.